Effective Christian Living

About the author

Born in Northern Ireland of humble, hard-working Christian parents. Received Christ at the age of 13. At 14 he was confined to bed for 5 months with a very serious illness, of which it was thought he would not recover, but during that illness he received a very clear call from God to devote his life to missionary work in Africa.

He trained in Glasgow and America. As a bachelor, worked among the so-called 'Coloured' people in South Africa. In 1952 married Isabel MacKenzie and they worked together in Africa from 1953 until 1986. Their invitations involved working with different missions and churches in village and student evangelism, Bible Studies for elders, teachers, pastors and missionaries, as well as writing material to help young Christians grow spiritually.

They worked in Kenya, Uganda, Tanzania, Zaire, Zambia, Zimbabwe, Swaziland, South Africa, as well as Malawi where the largest portion of their time was spent.

After retiring from 38 years of work in Africa, accepted a call to a Church of Scotland congregation in the Highlands of Scotland. Now doing pulpit supply, and involved in 3 month trips to Africa for special training of lay church workers.

Literature Produced

Following Jesus (For new converts)
Following Jesus (50 Studies for Theological Education by Extension)
The Church's First 30 Years in Malawi
Joseph Booth and John Chilembwe in Malawi
How to be a Happy Christian (A Correspondence Course)

Effective Christian Living

John Selfridge

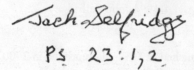

PS 23:1,2

Christian Focus Publications

I would like to thank my wife, Isabel, for her valuable assistance in checking over the manuscript.

©1994 John Selfridge
ISBN 1-85792-074-0

First published in 1994 and reprinted in 2000 by Christian Focus Publications, Geanies House, Fearn, Ross-shire, IV20 1TW, Scotland, Great Britain.

www.christianfocus.com

Printed and bound in Great Britain by Cox & Wyman, Reading, Berkshire

Cover design by Owen Daily

Scripture quotations, unless otherwise indicated, are from the *The Bible in Today's English Version*, published by the United Bible Societies.

Contents

FOREWORD by *Colin A M Sinclair* **8**

PREFACE **10**

STUDY ONE **11**
GOD WANTS EACH CHRISTIAN TO BEAR
SPIRITUAL FRUIT

STUDY TWO **15**
GOD'S PLAN FOR US TO BE FRUITFUL

STUDY THREE **20**
HOW DO WE BECOME FRUITFUL BRANCHES?

STUDY FOUR **25**
THE SPIRIT OF THE LORD JESUS IN THE FRUIT-
FUL BRANCH

STUDY FIVE **31**
A BRANCH MUST BE CLEAN

STUDY SIX **37**
THINGS WHICH MAKE A BRANCH UNCLEAN

STUDY SEVEN **44**
A FRUITFUL BRANCH MUST BE PRUNED

STUDY EIGHT **51**
THE BRANCH MUST ABIDE IN CHRIST

STUDY NINE 58
THE HOLY SPIRIT PRODUCES LOVE

STUDY TEN 63
THE HOLY SPIRIT BRINGS JOY

STUDY ELEVEN 70
THE HOLY SPIRIT BRINGS PEACE

STUDY TWELVE 76
THE HOLY SPIRIT BRINGS PATIENCE

STUDY THIRTEEN 81
THE HOLY SPIRIT BRINGS KINDNESS

STUDY FOURTEEN 87
THE HOLY SPIRIT BRINGS GOODNESS

STUDY FIFTEEN 93
THE HOLY SPIRIT PRODUCES FAITHFULNESS

STUDY SIXTEEN 100
THE HOLY SPIRIT PRODUCES HUMILITY

STUDY SEVENTEEN 107
THE HOLY SPIRIT BRINGS SELF-CONTROL

STUDY EIGHTEEN 114
SUMMARY OF THE FRUIT OF THE SPIRIT

STUDY NINETEEN **121**
GIFTS OF THE HOLY SPIRIT

STUDY TWENTY **128**
THE IMPORTANCE OF STUDYING GOD'S WORD

STUDY TWENTY ONE **134**
A FRUITFUL CHRISTIAN PRAYS

STUDY TWENTY TWO **140**
HOW SHOULD A FRUITFUL CHRISTIAN PRAY?

STUDY TWENTY THREE **146**
FISHING FOR SOULS

STUDY TWENTY FOUR **152**
METHODS OF WINNING PEOPLE

ANSWERS TO STUDY QUESTIONS **159**

FOREWORD

Almost 20 years ago as a young missionary in Africa, I had the privilege of staying for a week in the home of Jack and Isabel Selfridge in Malawi. This book reflects three characteristics of their ministry which was true then and has continued down through the years.

Firstly, it is *scriptural*. There is a tendency today to seek to bypass scripture in the search for spiritual growth. This book, which draws widely from the Bible, is written from the conviction that God still speaks through what he has spoken, and that God's word is living and active in both bringing people to faith and helping them to grow in Christ. It does not try to read out of the Bible what is not in it, but is content to lay open the plain sense of the word clearly and simply, believing it still has a transforming power for those who will read and respond to it.

Secondly, this book is *practical*. Earthed in illustrations drawn both from the author's own wide experience of Christian service and from his wider reading, it never fails to answer the question, 'So what?'. In very straightforward terms it works out the implications of the Christian faith in our daily life and service and underlines this through the very helpful study guide to each chapter.

Thirdly, it is *devotional*. Above all, this book seeks to deepen our daily walk with Jesus Christ, centred around the illustration of the vine and the branches in John 15. The author's desire is that we should 'know Christ better'. Those early disciples who were sent out to minister were first called 'to be with him' and our understanding of the Christian faith and our service to Christ arise from our abiding in him.

The Church in Africa instinctively turns to the Bible to see how the problems of daily life are to be met. This book encourages us in the West to do the same and to find joy and fruitfulness in the obedience of faith. I am glad to commend it for study as a resource to help our Christian nurture.

Colin A M Sinclair
General Director,
Scripture Union, Scotland

PREFACE

This series of Bible Studies on **Effective Christian Living** was prepared at the request of the Woman's Guild of the Nkhoma Synod of the Church of Central Africa Presbyterian, when I was a missionary in Malawi. The original studies were prepared in simple English, so that they could be published in the local language, Chichewa. The women wanted, during the course of a year, to have a study for each of their fortnightly meetings. Also, after they were prepared, I was asked by Trans World Radio, to broadcast the studies weekly, in their English service to Africa.

Now I have received some requests to have the series published in English. To do so I have had to decide if I should leave the English in its original simple form. Having spent 38 years as a missionary in a number of countries in Africa, previous studies I have prepared in English have been translated into as many as 30 other languages. I have tried, then, to leave the English in this series quite simple, to make it easier for anyone who might be involved in translating.

Also, to give the series a wider area in which they can be studied in English, I have used the Good News Bible, except where the King James Version (KJV), is noted. That is because the Good News Bible is the one mostly available to those where English is not the first language.

However, this simple form should make the book very acceptable in western countries for young Christians in Bible Classes and Discussion Groups, as well as in personal devotions.

My sincere prayer is that the Holy Spirit will use these studies for His own glory, and that through them, many will be enabled to grow in grace and lead spiritually fruitful lives.

John Selfridge
January 1994

STUDY ONE

GOD WANTS EACH CHRISTIAN TO BEAR SPIRITUAL FRUIT

Reading: Luke 13:6-9

Then Jesus told them this parable: 'There was once a man who had a fig-tree growing in his vineyard. He went looking for figs on it but found none.[7] So he said to his gardener, "Look, for three years I have been coming here looking for figs on this fig-tree, and I haven't found any. Cut it down! Why should it go on using up the soil?" [8]But the gardener answered, "Leave it alone, sir, just one more year; I will dig round it and put in some manure. [9]Then if the tree bears figs next year, so much the better; if not, then you can have it cut down." '

When we plant fruit trees in our gardens we want them to produce fruit. It would not please us if they only produced leaves and flowers. We must have fruit. The Lord Jesus said in John 15 that when we become Christians we are planted in this world, by His Father, the Heavenly Gardener, to bear spiritual fruit. In the same chapter, Jesus tells us that a Christian who bears spiritual fruit, brings glory and praise to His Father.

In our reading in Luke 13 Jesus gives us the account of a tree which did not bear fruit. Its owner was very disappointed, and after looking for fruit for three years, he told his gardener to cut it down. It was using space that

11

could be used for a fruitful tree. But the gardener begged the owner to allow him one more year to try and get the tree to produce fruit. He said he would dig round it and manure it, but if it failed to produce, he would cut it down.

Has the Lord been waiting a long time for fruit in our lives? Is He giving us an extension of time to allow us to fulfil God's plan? How sad it would be if we were like the tree which disappointed Jesus when He was walking along the road from Bethany to Jerusalem. He was hungry and went to a fig tree which was growing by the roadside, but found that there were no figs growing on the tree. We read the account in Matthew 21:18-20. Jesus said to the tree, 'You will never again bear fruit!' The tree withered at once and the disciples, who were with Jesus, were very surprised. What a calamity it would be if the Heavenly Gardener sees us as spiritually unfruitful, and pronounced the same command.

Why did Jesus explain about the tree that was given one more year to produce fruit? Why did He cause the other tree to wither? Was it not because He wanted to teach the lesson that Christians are like fruit trees planted in God's garden? He has planted us in this world to bear spiritual fruit, as Jesus points out so clearly in John 15. But if we do not bear fruit, then these two incidents point out that an unfruitful person is wasting space in the church of Jesus Christ!

In Galatians 5:22, 23 Paul describes the fruit that the Lord wants us to produce. It is a fruit that is made up of nine parts - love, joy, peace, patience, kindness, goodness, faithfulness, humility, and self-control. Notice that the Bible does not say the 'fruits' of the Spirit, but the 'fruit'. These are not all separate fruits, but all part of the one fruit.

When we meet God, how sad it will be for anyone who has nothing to give to God but leaves, instead of fruit. If we have the fruit of the Spirit in our lives, it results in others being brought to Jesus.

The following poem, describing a dream, illustrates this truth, because Jesus said, 'Pray to the owner of the harvest that he will send out workers to gather in his harvest' (Matthew 9:38; Luke 10:2).

The time of the harvest was ended,
And the summer of life was gone,
When in from the fields came the reapers,
Called home by the dip of the sun;
I saw them each bearing a burden
Of toilsomely ingathered sheaves;
They brought them in love to the Master,
But I could bring nothing but leaves.
The years that He gave I had wasted,
Nor thought I how soon they would fly,
While others toiled hard for the harvest,
I carelessly let them slip by;
I idled about without purpose,
Nor cared I, but now how it grieves;
While others brought fruit to their Master,
I found I had nothing but leaves.

Then soon from my dream I was wakened,
And sad was my heart, for I knew

That though my life's day was not over,
Ere long I should bid it adieu.
I started in shame and in sorrow,
I turned from the sin that deceives;
Henceforth I must toil for the Saviour
Or maybe bring nothing but leaves.

Questions

1. What did Jesus say would glorify God?

2. Why did the owner of the vineyard want the unfruitful tree cut down?

3. Why do you think Jesus used this parable?

4. What is the lesson we learn from the gardener asking for one more year in which to try to get the tree to become fruitful?

5. What lesson do we learn from the tree, which Jesus said would never bear any more fruit?

6. Why did Paul use the singular for Fruit of the Spirit, and not Fruits of the Spirit?

7. What does God use in our lives to attract others to follow Jesus?

8. What would make us very sad when we stand before God?

9. What does the harvest story in the dream, teach us about the use of our time?

10. Can you give one of the references where Jesus asks us to pray for more labourers to be sent into the Lord's harvest field?

STUDY TWO

GOD'S PLAN FOR US TO BE FRUITFUL

Reading: John 15:1-8

'I am the real vine, and my Father is the gardener. ²He breaks off every branch in me that does not bear fruit, and he prunes every branch that does bear fruit, so that it will be clean and bear more fruit. ³You have been made clean already by the teaching I have given you. ⁴Remain united to me, and I will remain united to you. A branch cannot bear fruit by itself; it can do so only if it remains in the vine. In the same way you cannot bear fruit unless you remain in me.

'⁵I am the vine, and you are the branches. Whoever remains in me, and I in him, will bear much fruit; for you can do nothing without me. ⁶Whoever does not remain in me is thrown out like a branch and dries up; such branches are gathered up and thrown into the fire, where they are burnt. ⁷If you remain in me and my words remain in you, then you will ask for anything you wish, and you shall have it. ⁸My Father's glory is shown by your bearing much fruit; and in this way you become my disciples.'

God is a wonderful designer! We see how He has put the sun, moon, stars, and planets in space. They all keep time like a gigantic clock, so that those who study the science of astronomy, can tell us exactly when the sun will rise and set on any day, hundreds of years from now. How can they give such accurate time so far ahead? It is because the Lord has designed the perfect time plan that keeps these heavenly bodies from varying one ten thousandth of a second in ten thousand years!

We also see God's wonderful plan in vegetables, trees and flowers, enabling them to reproduce through the seeds in their fruit. If our Heavenly Father has designed such a wonderful plan so that the plant world can produce fruit, then His plan for us as Christians to produce spiritual fruit must be even more wonderful. The fruit which plants produce does not last, but spiritual fruit is everlasting and will continue for ever in the heavenly home.

1. What is God's plan?

In our reading from John chapter 15 we find that Jesus likens Himself to a vine, and He said that Christians are branches in that Vine. When we invite the Lord Jesus into our lives as our Saviour, Paul tells us in 2 Corinthians 5:17, that we become new persons. We are then joined to Jesus as a branch in a vine. When we are joined to Him, the Holy Spirit flows from Him into us, just as the sap from a tree, or a vine, flows into the branches. It is the Holy Spirit in us that produces the spiritual fruit Paul tells us about in Galatians 5:22, 23, as we saw in study one. Jesus also pointed out in John chapter 15 that the Heavenly Father is the Gardener! He is watching over us, cleansing, pruning and protecting us, so that we can produce much fruit. That is the plan that God has made for each Christian. What a wonderful and important position we hold when we become Christians. Each one of us, as a branch, is grafted into the Heavenly Vine, the Lord Jesus.

2. We must fit into God's plan

In our reading, Jesus warns us that we must continue to remain in Him. A branch separated from a tree cannot produce fruit. Jesus said in verse 5, 'For you can do nothing without me.' He went on to say in verse 6, 'Whoever does not remain in me, is thrown out like a branch and dries up: such branches are gathered up and thrown into the fire, where they are burnt.'

We see many nominal church members who are dry and withered. They are not dwelling in Jesus day by day. Because they are separated from Him, the sap of the Holy Spirit is not flowing into their lives. They are interested in things which grieve the Lord Jesus, and so are disobedient. They do not produce spiritual fruit. Jesus said, 'If you obey my commands, you will remain in my love, just as I have obeyed my Father's commands and remain in his love' (verse 10). If we do not obey Him, we cannot be fruitful Christians.

3. What happens if we do not fit into God's plan?

In the Bible there are many warnings against failing to fit into the plan that the Lord has made for us. First, let us look in the Old Testament. In Psalm 80:8-13, we are told that the people of God were like a vine that was wasted, because they disobeyed Him. In Isaiah 5:4, God asks, 'Is there anything I failed to do for it (His vineyard)? Then why did it produce sour grapes and not the good grapes I expected?' The Children of Israel only produced 'sour grapes' because the people did not respond to God's commands, and obey Him. Sour grapes was God's description of their sinful ways.

Again God spoke to the Israelites and said, in Jeremiah 2:21, 'I planted you like a choice vine from the very best seed. But look what you have become! You are like a rotten, worthless vine'. That is what happens in the life of a person who has the name of being a Christian, but who is not willing to fit into God's plan. He or she bears the wrong kind of fruit - 'rotten, worthless' fruit is fruit that does not have the quality that it should have. It forms the kind of fruit that Paul tells us about in Galatians 5:20, 21, which includes strife, jealousy, envy, anger, selfishness, party spirit, witchcraft (or the occult), adultery, drunkenness, and other evil things.

In Acts chapter 5 we read about two church members whose fruit was evil. They lied to the Holy Spirit, and both of them dropped dead in the church service. They promised God a certain sum of money, but they kept part of it for themselves. We read of a man called Demas who loved the present world so much that he left the work God had given him to do, 2 Timothy 4:10.

We see then, that God has a wonderful plan for each one of us to produce spiritual fruit. But we must 'live' in Jesus every day by obediently keeping the commands He has given us. If we do not abide, or remain in Him, then we will wither, and will be bearing the kinds of fruit we read about when God was angry with His people in the Old Testament, or the kind Paul tells us about in the above verses.

Questions

1. Name two things God has planned which show how wonderfully He can design?

2. What design is even more wonderful?

3. How do we become a branch in Jesus, the Vine?

4. Who flows from Jesus into us when we are branches?

5. What happens when the Holy Spirit flows through us?

6. What are the verses which describe the Fruit of the Spirit?

7. What part does the Heavenly Father take in helping us to bear fruit?

8. How do we know that we cannot bear fruit without remaining in Jesus?

9. What must we do if we want to remain in the love of Jesus?

10. Which verses tell us the kind of fruit produced by those who are not Christians?

STUDY THREE

HOW DO WE BECOME FRUITFUL BRANCHES?

Reading: Ezekiel 36:24-30

I will take you from every nation and country and bring you back to your own land. [25]I will sprinkle clean water on you and make you clean from all your idols and everything else that has defiled you. [26]I will give you a new heart and a new mind. I will take away your stubborn heart of stone and give you an obedient heart. [27]I will put my spirit in you and I will see to it that you follow my laws and keep all the commands I have given you. [28]Then you will live in the land I gave your ancestors. You will be my people, and I will be your God. [29]I will save you from everything that defiles you. I will command the corn to be plentiful, so that you will not have any more famines. [30]I will increase the yield of your fruit-trees and your fields, so that there will be no more famines to disgrace you among the nations.

In our last study we saw the wonderful plan God has made for us so that we can bear spiritual fruit. You will remember that it is only when we remain in Christ, that we can produce fruit. The Holy Spirit flows from Him into us like sap flows from a tree into the branches. In this study we will see how one becomes a branch in the Lord Jesus, the Heavenly Vine.

If the Holy Spirit flows from Jesus into us, then we will receive the nature of Jesus. The branch of a tree has the same nature as the tree. That is why Paul wrote, 'Let this mind be in you which was also in Christ Jesus' (Philippians 2:5 [KJV]). In 1 Corinthians 2:16 he also writes, 'We have the mind of Christ'. Paul also urges the Christians in Rome not to be conformed to this world but to let God transform them inwardly by a complete change of mind. Then they would be able to know the will of God - what is good and pleasing to Him, and is perfect (Romans 12:2).

Because of the sin of our first parents in the Garden of Eden, when we are born into this world we do not have the same nature as Jesus. We read in Psalm 51:5, 'I have been evil from the day I was born; from the time I was conceived, I have been sinful'. We also read in Romans 3:23, 'Everyone has sinned and is far away from God's saving presence'. How then can we be changed so that we will have the same nature as Jesus, seeing we are born with a sinful nature? How may we, as branches, become like Jesus our Vine?

We must be changed

Jesus told Nicodemus in John 3:7, 'Do not be surprised because I tell you that you must all be born again'. Nicodemus thought Jesus implied that he had to have a new body. He thought Jesus meant that he had to become a baby and be born from his mother again. But Jesus explained that it was not his body that needed to be born again but the spirit inside him. When our body does sinful things it is not the fault of the body, but it is because there is a sinful spirit, or nature, inside us, which uses our bodies. So Jesus said to Nicodemus in verse 6, 'A person is born physically of human parents, but he is born spiritually of the Spirit'. It is the Holy Spirit who gives birth to a new spirit within us.

I asked a teacher in Africa, 'How long have you been a Christian?' 'I was born a Christian,' he answered. He explained that he was born a Christian because his parents were Christians. I told him that I too had Christian parents, but that did not make me a Christian. I had done many things that I should not have done, because of a wrong spirit. I had to come to Jesus and ask Him to forgive, and change me. Then the teacher admitted, 'I too am a big sinner. I have been planning to leave my wife and go off with another woman. I see that I also need to be born again.' As we prayed together he admitted his sinful ways, and asked for forgiveness. He trusted the Lord to make him into a new person. Today he is a minister and bearing fruit for the Lord Jesus.

How can we be changed?

The angel which came to Joseph to tell him that Mary would have a child by the Holy Spirit, said, 'You will name him Jesus - because he will save his people from their sins' (Matthew 1:21). How then does Jesus save His people from their sins? How does He change men and women and impart His nature?

Jesus states in Revelation 3:20, 'I stand at the door and knock; if anyone hears my voice and opens the door, I will come into his house and eat with him, and he will eat with me'. That is how we are changed. Jesus wants to come into our hearts, through the Holy Spirit, and live there. He then gives us a new spirit which replaces our old sinful spirit.

The Lord tells us about this great change in Ezekiel 36:26, 27. 'I will give you a new heart and a new mind... I will put my Spirit in you and I will see to it that you follow my laws and keep all the commandments I have given you.' Paul described the great change that takes place when the Lord Jesus comes to live in us: 'When anyone is joined to Christ, he is a new being; the old is gone, the new has come' (2 Corinthians 5:17).

We have seen then that we are to be branches in Jesus, the Heavenly Vine, and that the branch must have the same nature as the Vine. That means that we must have the mind of Christ, with His nature and Spirit within us. That is why Peter wrote in 2 Peter 1:4, 'He has given us the very great and precious gifts He promised, so that by means of these gifts you may escape from the destructive lust that is in the world, and may come to share the divine nature'.

It is not enough, then, just to be a church member, if we want to be a branch that bears spiritual fruit. We must have the Lord Jesus dwelling within. Then He will produce fruit through us by His Holy Spirit. Is the Lord Jesus living in your life? Have you opened the door and said to Him, 'Come in'?

Questions

1. Describe the kind of a mind a Christian should have.

2. What does it mean to be 'conformed to the world' in Romans 12:2?

3. What happens when we receive the mind of Christ?

4. Explain what Paul says happens when we are in Christ?

5. Discuss the kind of nature, or mind, we have when we are born.

6. Why did Jesus tell Nicodemus that he had to be 'born again'?

7. What did Nicodemus think Jesus meant by the New Birth?

8. Explain what Jesus meant by the New Birth.

9. How does Ezekiel explain what happens when a person is born again?

10. If a person's parents are Christians, does that mean that person is born a Christian?

STUDY FOUR

THE SPIRIT OF THE LORD JESUS IN THE FRUITFUL BRANCH

Reading: John 3:1-15

There was a Jewish leader named Nicodemus, who belonged to the party of the Pharisees. [2]One night he went to Jesus and said to him, 'Rabbi, we know that you are a teacher sent by God. No one could perform the miracles you are doing unless God were with him.'

[3]Jesus answered, 'I am telling you the truth: no one can see the Kingdom of God unless he is born again.'

[4]"How can a grown man be born again?' Nicodemus asked. 'He certainly cannot enter his mother's womb and be born a second time!'

[5]'I am telling you the truth,' replied Jesus. 'No one can enter the Kingdom of God unless he is born of water and the Spirit. [6]A person is born physically of human parents, but he is born spiritually of the Spirit. [7]Do not be surprised because I tell you that you must all be born again. [8]The wind blows wherever it wishes; you hear the sound it makes, but you do not know where it comes from or where it is going. It is like that with everyone who is born of the Spirit.'

[9]"How can this be?' asked Nicodemus.

[10]Jesus answered, 'You are a great teacher in Israel, and you don't know this? [11]I am telling you the truth: we speak of what we know and report what we have seen, yet none of you is willing to accept our message.

[12] You do not believe me when I tell you about the things of this world; how will you ever believe me, then, when I tell you about the things of heaven? [13] And no one has ever gone up to heaven except the Son of Man, who came down from heaven.'

[14] As Moses lifted up the bronze snake on a pole in the desert, in the same way the Son of Man must be lifted up. [15] So that everyone who believes in him may have eternal life.'

In our last study we saw that we, as Christians, must be fruitful branches, and that the branches must have the same nature as Jesus, the Vine. To have the same nature as Jesus we must be 'born again'. We read about the new birth in the above scripture reading. We are born again when the Lord Jesus comes into our lives to reside. The Bible states that He comes into our hearts, but of course that is not the organ which pumps the blood through our bodies. The Bible means the centre of our desires - where our will controls the thoughts we think, the words we say, and the things we do. When Jesus comes in, His Spirit imparts to us His nature which transforms the desires that control us. We become new persons in Christ (2 Corinthians 5:17).

In this study let us look at four things which prepare our hearts as a home for the Spirit of the Lord Jesus, so that we can be fruitful branches.

1. We must be sorry for our sins
We saw from Scripture, in a former study, that we are all born sinners. We have all done things that we should not

have done. We must be sorry that we have done the things which grieve the Holy Spirit. In 2 Corinthians 7:8-11 (KJV), Paul writes about two kinds of sorrow, or sadness. Some people are only sorry because they have been found out, and are afraid of being punished. Paul calls that the 'sorrow of the world'. But true sorrow is the sadness which comes to us when we realise that we have grieved the Lord, who loves us so much. Paul calls that 'Godly sorrow'. That kind of sorrow makes us hate our sins and want to forsake them and find forgiveness.

2. We must confess our sins to God

We read in 1 John 1:9, 'If we confess our sins to God, he will keep his promise and do what is right; he will forgive us our sins and purify us from all our wrongdoing'. Many people try to hide their sins. They are like a man I once saw in Africa, who found a spot of leprosy on his chest. Instead of going to a doctor to seek a cure, he had a tattoo of a flower put on top of the spot to hide it. He knew that if people in his village found out that he was a leper they would chase him from the village. He thought he was clever in being able to hide his disease in that way. But very soon the leprosy came out on other parts of his body, including his face. He could not hide it any longer, but by that time he was very ill, and I understand, died of his disease.

Sin is like leprosy! It may be hidden for a short time, but the Bible says, 'Be sure your sin will find you out' (Numbers 32:23, KJV). The Lord Jesus will not allow His Holy Spirit to live in a life where there is hidden sin.

You remember Zacchaeus, when Jesus wanted to go

to his home (Luke 19:1-9). Zacchaeus admitted his sins to Jesus. He said, 'Listen, sir! I will give half my belongings to the poor, and if I have cheated anyone, I will pay him back four times as much.' Zacchaeus was really sorry for the wrong he had done and Jesus forgave him right away. He said, 'Salvation has come to this house today.' Jesus did not wait until Zacchaeus had seen all the people he had wronged. As soon as he was willing to really repent, he was forgiven.

When we confess our sins to God, and are willing to put things right with those we have wronged, God forgives us. However, we are only forgiven because Jesus died on the cross and took our punishment. Putting wrongs right with others cannot merit forgiveness. We only do that because of the Godly sorrow in our hearts. Even if we gave back things we had stolen we would still be a thief. Only God can blot out the guilt of sin, because Jesus died for us.

3. We must leave our sins

It is not enough to keep confessing our sins to God and then going back and doing them again! In Proverbs 28:13, we read, 'You will never succeed in life if you try to hide your sins. Confess them and give them up; then God will show mercy to you'. Some people go to church and confess sins once a week to a priest, but they go back and do the same things again the following week! That is not real sorrow for sin, because they are not willing to forsake their sins. Others confess sins each night, but do not really want to leave them. Of course, we must always pray, as Jesus told us to do, 'forgive us the wrongs we have done' (Matthew 6:12), because we all come short of absolute perfection, but that is different from continuing habitually to do the things which grieve the Lord. 'Sin must not be your master,' Paul wrote in Romans 6:14. John writes, 'Whoever is a child of God does not continue to sin' (1 John 3:9).

4. We must trust God to forgive us

We have read in 1 John 1:9, that if we confess our sins God will forgive us. We have also read in Proverbs 28:13, that if we confess and give up our sins we will find mercy and be forgiven. But God is holy and pure, how then can He forgive us? He can forgive us because Jesus came into this world and received the punishment we should have received. Isaiah wrote in chapter 53, verses 4 to 6, that He was wounded for us, and that the Lord made the punishment we all deserved, fall on Him.

Jesus died for us. If we are sorry for our sins, confess them to God, and really want to leave them, then we can ask for forgiveness. God cannot break His promises. He loved us so much that He sent the Lord Jesus to save us from our sins (Matthew 1:21). And as John tells us, He will keep His promise and forgive. We must then have faith to believe that He has forgiven us when we ask Him, and that His Holy Spirit has come to dwell in us. When we have faith to believe that He has forgiven us, we will experience what Paul describes in Romans 8:16, 'God's Spirit joins himself to our spirits to declare that we are God's children'. We then receive an assurance that all the past has been blotted out, and will never be remembered against us any more for ever. We are justified - God looks on us as if we had never sinned, because Jesus has carried our sins away.

By taking the four steps described in this study, we become branches in the Lord Jesus, and the Holy Spirit from Him is then able to produce fruit in our lives.

Questions

1. Discuss how we, as branches, receive the nature of the Lord Jesus.

2. Explain what the Bible means when it states that Jesus comes into our hearts.

3. Can you remember the four things that prepare us to be a home in which the Holy Spirit can dwell?

4. Where does Paul mention two kinds of 'sorrow', or sadness?

5. Discuss the difference between these two types of 'sorrow'.

6. To whom should we confess our sins?

7. Is it all right to confess sin week by week, and keep going back to commit it again?

8. Discuss what it means to believe in Jesus.

9. Can we be sure that we are forgiven by God, and that we are His children? Discuss Romans 8:16.

10. If asked to explain the word 'justification', how would you answer?

STUDY FIVE

A BRANCH MUST BE CLEAN

Reading: 2 Timothy 2:19, 20

> But the solid foundation that God has laid cannot be
> shaken; and on it are written these words: 'The Lord
> knows those who are his' and 'Whoever says that he
> belongs to the Lord must turn away from wrongdoing.'
> ²⁰ In a large house there are dishes and bowls of all
> kinds: some are made of silver and gold, others of wood
> and clay; some are for special occasions, others for
> ordinary use.

We have seen in our studies so far that the Heavenly
Gardener wants us to be fruitful. We must be branches in
the Lord Jesus, who is the Vine, so that we can produce
fruit. In this study we will see that a branch must be clean
- all the disease and fungi of sin must be removed and
cleansed.

Jesus said in John 15:3, 'You have been made clean
already by the teaching I have given you'. In the above
Scripture reading, Paul told Timothy that one must be
clean, and always ready for the Lord to use. If there are
wrong things in our lives, we will not be fruitful. Like a
fungus on the branch of a fruit tree, the wrong things are
parasites. They absorb strength from the branch, hinder
growth and the production of spiritual fruit.

In our gardens we find that diseases attack our fruit

trees. Very often a fungus grows on the branches and takes away strength from the branch. The branch becomes weak. Sinful things in our lives are like fungi. They cause us to be weak and unfruitful. The Bible teaches us that we need to be cleansed.

King David needed cleansing

You will remember that King David sinned. He committed adultery with Bathsheba

When he found out that she was pregnant, he arranged for her husband to be murdered. He was able to hide his two-fold sin until after the baby was born. Then the prophet, Nathan, came to David and challenged him about his sins (2 Samuel 12). David became honest with the prophet and admitted that he had sinned, and that he was unclean. In Psalm 51 we read his prayer for cleansing. He prayed, 'Wash away all my evil and make me clean from my sin! I recognise my faults... create a pure heart in me, O God... Give me again the joy that comes from your salvation... then will I teach sinners your commands and they will turn back to you.'

David knew that while he was unclean with sin, he could not turn sinners back to God. So Christians who have sin hidden in their hearts, are not able to work for God. They cannot produce the fruit of the Holy Spirit until, like David, sin is confessed and forgiveness and cleansing takes place.

Isaiah admitted that he was unclean

We read in Isaiah chapter 6 that he had a vision of God. He saw Him sitting on His throne. Around Him were heavenly beings calling, 'Holy, holy, holy, the Lord almighty is holy!'. As Isaiah saw the holiness of God, and compared the way he lived and the way he spoke, he saw how unclean he was. He then cried out to God, 'There is no hope for me, I am doomed because every word that passes my lips is sinful, and I live among a people whose every word is sinful'. When he confessed his unclean state to God his lips were touched with a burning object, by one of the heavenly beings, who said, 'This has touched your lips, and now your guilt is gone, and your sins are forgiven'.

Immediately after that he heard the Lord ask, 'Whom shall I send? Who will be our messenger?'. Then Isaiah answered, 'I will go! Send me!' Isaiah was not able to go to work for God until he was cleansed from the unclean things in his life. But what an abundantly fruitful life he had after that! Although he lived about 700 years before Christ came to this world, he was used by God to announce the good news of the Saviour who was coming to save people from their sins. He told how Jesus would suffer and die, and take the punishment we deserved, so we could be forgiven (Isaiah 53).

The disciples needed to be cleansed
Jesus spent three years teaching and training His disciples, but we read that sinful things remained in their hearts. In Luke 22:24, we are told that one day Jesus found them arguing. One was saying that he was the greatest disciple, and another was saying, 'No, I am better than you are'. They had pride, and James tells us that God resists the proud, but gives grace to the humble (James 4:6).

They were also ambitious. They wanted to be given important places in God's kingdom. James and John said to Jesus, 'When you sit on your throne in your glorious Kingdom, we want you to let us sit with you, one at your right hand and one at your left' (Mark 10:37). When the other ten disciples heard that James and John were pressing for such favours, they became angry and jealous (v 41). Jesus then pointed out to them that in His kingdom the one that is greatest is the one that is least, and is the servant of all.

We see trouble like that in our church organisations today. Some want prominent positions, but not with the sincere motive of serving the Lord. They want to be looked upon as important people. They are proud like the disciples were. Then someone else who wanted a position and did not get it, becomes jealous, and starts to criticise, and soon false rumours begin to divide the fellowship of a church.

Pride in the lives of the disciples also made them weak in times of temptation, although they thought they were very strong followers of Christ. Jesus tried to warn them that they would all run away and leave Him, but they said that they would never run away, even if they had to die with Him (Matthew 26:31-35). Peter especially boasted that he would die with Christ, rather than run away from Him. Jesus had to give him a warning: 'Before the cock crows tonight, you will say three times that you do not know me.' But he would not listen.

When the soldiers came to arrest Jesus, all the disciples ran away and left Him. They were full of fear. Peter told lies, cursed and swore that he did not know Jesus.

Jesus knew that the disciples were unclean, with their pride, ambition and fear. He knew that unless they were cleansed from these things, they would never be able to launch His church, and look after it. Their lives would be spiritually unfruitful. Because of that, He told them in Luke 24:49, 'You must wait in the city until the power from above comes down upon you'. And in Acts 1:8, He promised that they would receive power when the Holy Spirit was given to them.

The disciples took His advice and spent ten days in prayer, waiting until they received the Holy Spirit. We are not given details of what happened in the upstairs room where they prayed. But we can imagine that there must have been honest confession to God, and expression to one another of their failures, fear, and denial of Christ. It must have been a time of great cleansing in their lives.

As we read through the Acts of the Apostles, we find that the accounts there are really Acts of the Holy Spirit through the apostles! A great change took place when they were filled with the Holy Spirit, and received His power. They were able to win many people for Jesus, as they witnessed to them about the death and resurrection of Christ - the Saviour of all who would believe. Pride, ambition, jealousy and fear were no longer robbing them of spiritual fruit. We read in Acts 4:32, 33, 'The group of believers was one in mind and heart... with great power, the apostles gave witness to the resurrection of the Lord Jesus, and God poured rich blessings on them all'.

The day they were filled with the Holy Spirit, they were able to influence 3000 people on the street in Jerusalem, to accept Christ as their Saviour and Lord. We read that people were added to the church daily. What wonderful fruitful branches those early Christians became when they received their cleansing. That is the requirement for all Christians, and John tells us how it takes place in our lives. 'If we live in the light - just as He is in the light - then we have fellowship with one another, and the blood of Jesus, His Son, purifies us from every sin' (1 John 1:7).

Questions

1. Why are sinful things like disease on the branch of a fruit tree?

2. What reasons did David give for wanting to be cleansed?

3. Discuss the confession of Isaiah. What did he mean by unclean lips?

4. Why do you think Isaiah did not hear God's request for a messenger until after he was cleansed?

5. Name three things which would have hindered the disciples from being clean witnesses.

6. What shows that they were ashamed of Jesus, and frightened to stand up for Him?

7. Discuss the ways in which Christians are ashamed of Jesus now.

8. In what way did Jesus promise to send power to the disciples, so they could witness.

9. Why could the Acts of the Apostles have been called, 'The Acts of the Holy Spirit'?

10. Discuss how you think the disciples spent the ten days in the upper room.

STUDY SIX

THINGS WHICH MAKE A BRANCH UNCLEAN

Reading: Psalm 51:1-13

Be merciful to me, O God,
  because of your constant love.
Because of your great mercy
  wipe away my sins!
²Wash away all my evil
  and make me clean from my sin!

³I recognise my faults;
  I am always conscious of my sins.
⁴I have sinned against you - only against you -
  and done what you consider evil.
So you are right in judging me;
  you are justified in condemning me.
⁵I have been evil from the day I was born;
  from the time I was conceived, I have been sinful.

⁶Sincerity and truth are what you require;
  fill my mind with your wisdom.
⁷Remove my sin, and I will be clean;
  wash me, and I will be whiter than snow.
⁸Let me hear the sounds of joy and gladness;
  and though you have crushed me and broken me,
  I will be happy once again.
⁹Close your eyes to my sins

and wipe out all my evil.
[10]Create a pure heart in me, O God,
and put a new and loyal spirit in me.
[11]Do not banish me from your presence;
do not take your holy spirit away from me.
[12]Give me again the joy that comes from your salvation,
and make me willing to obey you.
[13]Then I will teach sinners your commands,
and they will turn back to you.

In our last study we saw that David, Isaiah, and the disciples had to be cleansed: they could not produce spiritual fruit until the wrong things had been taken out of their lives. Now we come to the very important question: what are the things in our lives that make us unclean? What things would hinder us from bearing fruit for the Lord? These are very important questions, so let us consider them.

Anger

Paul wrote in Ephesians 4:26, 'Do not let your anger lead you into sin'. If one says angry words, or does things because anger has caused loss of control of one's actions, that person will not be a fruitful Christian. David said in Psalm 37:8, 'Don't give in to worry or anger'. And in Proverbs 14:17, we read, 'People with a hot temper do foolish things'.

I have a friend who was a missionary doctor in Africa. One day he got very angry with a member of his staff. He was so angry that he lost control of his words, and said many things he should not have said. After he stopped shouting, his African assistant said to him, 'I thought you were a Christian'. The doctor was very much ashamed. He saw that he was unclean, just like Isaiah who cried out when he had a vision of God, 'I am doomed because every word that passes from my lips is sinful', as we saw in our last study. The doctor rushed to his house, as soon as he could get off duty, and shutting himself in his room, he knelt before God, crying for forgiveness and cleansing. He prayed that the Lord would remove the anger. God answered his prayer, and he became a very successful worker for the Lord, not only in the field of medicine, but also as a fruitful witness for Christ.

Dishonesty

If we are deceitful about anything, it grieves the Holy Spirit. Paul wrote to the Colossian Christians in chapter 3, verse 9, 'Do not lie to one another, for you have taken off the old self with its habits'.

There was great trouble in a congregation. Many members were being suspended for sinful things. The minister was very discouraged, so he called his congregation's leaders together. He said to them, 'The Lord is no longer blessing us in this congregation. There is something grieving the Holy Spirit. Let us meet every day to pray until God reveals to us what is wrong, and why the Holy Spirit is being hindered.'

After they had prayed daily for about six weeks, an elder stood up in the prayer meeting and said, 'I am the one to blame for the hindrance to the spiritual life of this congregation. I have grieved the Holy Spirit. I was asked by one of the congregation, just before his death, to sell his cattle and to give the money to his wife, but I did not give her all the money. I put some of it into my own pocket. Tomorrow I will go and give her the rest of the money.'

As soon as he confessed his dishonesty in the prayer meeting, other elders and deacons were convicted, and with tears, also admitted wrong things in their lives.

After that the congregation was revived, and 3000 new members were added during the next year. Twelve new meeting places had to be built to accommodate the new converts in the area. If a leader in a congregation is dishonest, not only is he unfruitful in his own life, but the congregation where he is a leader is hindered from bearing spiritual fruit. Just as Achan's dishonesty when he stole in Jericho, and hid the loot, caused the whole of the Israelites to suffer defeat, so this dishonest elder hindered victory. As God told Joshua, 'I will not stay with you any longer unless you destroy the things you were ordered not to take! You cannot stand against your enemies until you get rid of these things!' (Joshua 7:12, 13). When there is sin in the church, there is spiritual defeat.

Debt

In Romans 13:8, we are commanded, 'Owe no man anything' (KJV). But some church members borrow money and never return it. Others take goods on credit and fail to pay their bills. A storekeeper told a visiting minister who was holding special evangelistic meetings in a church in the town, 'One of the members in that church got a shirt from my store a long time ago and never makes any attempt to pay for it. If that is Christianity I do not want to have anything to do with it'.

At the next service the visiting minister announced from the pulpit, 'I am told by a storekeeper in this town that a member of this church has bought a shirt, a long time ago, and has never paid for it. How can we expect God to bless our special services if there is such dishonesty in the church? If that shirt is not paid for tomorrow, I will announce the member's name and address from this pulpit. The next day 28 shirts were paid for in the different stores in that town! All these people had owed money, but did not know to which one the minister referred! Debt makes church members unclean in God's sight, if they are not doing all they can to pay.

Witchcraft

In Galatians 5:20, we are told that those who practise witchcraft will not possess the kingdom of God. When we think of witchcraft, we think of witchdoctors, but witchcraft is not confined to witchdoctors. The Israelites were warned by God not to practise black magic, or call on the evil spirits for aid, or go to fortune-tellers, wizards, or the spirits of the dead. For all these, they were told, were an abomination to the Lord (Deuteronomy 18:10-12).

In spite of the many warnings in the Bible against what we now know as the occult, there are church members who try to find out what the future holds for them, by consulting so-called fortune-tellers. They have their palms read, or they consult horoscopes, or someone who gazes into a crystal ball. Others seek through mediums to talk to the spirits of the dead. Jesus warned us not to consult such people. He said, 'False prophets will appear; they will perform great miracles and wonders in order to deceive God's chosen people, if possible... don't go there' (Matthew 24:24, 26).

One day when I was working in Africa I went to a witchdoctor's village. While there I prayed that God would destroy the power of his charms and other witch-craft items, because we are told in Ephesians 1:21 that Jesus has been set far above all other power and might and dominion. I knew that witchdoctor got his power from Satan. It was five years before I saw the witchdoctor again. When we met he asked me for medicine, as he was not feeling well. I asked him why he did not use his own medicine. He replied, 'From that day when you visited my village, my medicine lost all its power'. Jesus is stronger than Satan, and it grieves the Holy Spirit if church members think that these servants of Satan can help them better than He can. They are putting another 'god' before the Lord, and that makes them unclean.

Adultery and other sexual offences

In Galatians chapter 5, mentioned earlier, we also read that those who commit adultery and fornication will not inherit the kingdom of God. We have seen how king David sinned in that way. It is sad that in these days many church members have been guilty of these and other similar sins, and even church leaders are guilty. I know of a group of 20 women who meet in England. They were all wives of ministers who have been unfaithful to them and have gone off with other women!

Let us all examine ourselves then and allow the Holy

Spirit to show us if there is any fungus of sin on us as a branch that should be bearing fruit. Is there anger, dishonesty, debt, trust in fortune-tellers, sexual immorality, or any other unclean thing in our lives? If so let us claim 1 John 1:7-9.

Questions

1. How does anger hinder a person from serving Jesus?

2. How does Proverbs describe the kind of things an angry person does?

3. Is it all right for a Christian to tell a so-called 'white' lie?

4. Discuss what may happen in a congregation if a church leader is dishonest.

5. Explain what happened to the Children of Israel when Achan stole.

6. What is the result if a Christian fails to pay his, or her, bills, or other debts?

7. Why is it wrong to depend on horoscopes, or consult fortune-tellers?

8. Why is it wrong for unmarried couples to live as man and wife?

9. What is the difference between fornication and adultery?

10. Do you remember a reference in Scripture which tells us that we can be cleansed from all unrighteousness?

STUDY SEVEN

A FRUITFUL BRANCH MUST BE PRUNED

Reading: Colossians 3:12-17

You are the people of God; he loved you and chose you for his own. So then, you must clothe yourselves with compassion, kindness, humility, gentleness, and patience. [13]Be tolerant with one another and forgive one another whenever any of you has a complaint against someone else. You must forgive one another just as the Lord has forgiven you. [14]And to all these qualities add love, which binds all things together in perfect unity. [15]The peace that Christ gives is to guide you in the decisions you make; for it is to this peace that God has called you together in the one body. And be thankful. [16]Christ's message in all its richness must live in your hearts. Teach and instruct each other with all wisdom. Sing psalms, hymns, and sacred songs; sing to God with thanksgiving in your hearts. [17]Everything you do or say, then, should be done in the name of the Lord Jesus, as you give thanks through him to God the Father.

We have studied that as branches in Jesus, the Heavenly Vine, we must be clean. We must be cleansed from sin, or we will not bear spiritual fruit (John 15:3). But there is something else that is very important. If we want to be fruitful Christians, we must be pruned.

Jesus said in John 15, that His Father is the Gardener, and that He prunes every branch that bears fruit, so that it will produce more fruit. What a capable Gardener we have to look after us. One we can trust with the pruning knife! Cleansing takes away the bad things in our lives; pruning takes away some of the good things in our lives. A gardener who prunes a fruit tree in his garden knows that if there are too many twigs and offshoots on his tree it will produce inferior fruit, so he has to cut off some of the good growth. It is like that in our Christian lives. We can spend so much time and energy on good things, that better and more profitable things are neglected. We can be covered with a lot of leaves of activity and service, but produce very little fruit.

In Hebrews 12:1, we are told to put away everything that gets in the way as well as the sin that would hinder us. So it is not only sin that must go out of our lives, but anything that hinders us from having the greatest spiritual success in bearing fruit. An athlete running in a race, throws off everything that is unnecessary. It would be foolish to run in heavy boots and an overcoat. Boots and overcoats are good for certain occasions, but not for running in a race. In our lives good things can be a hindrance if they are used at the wrong time. They can use up too much energy that should be used in a more fruitful activity. Let us examine some of the things that, if not used properly, can hinder us from bearing the fruit of the Holy Spirit, as listed in Galatians 5:22, 23.

Time
For instance, time can be misused. Time is a very precious thing. We have about 15 or 16 hours each day when we are not sleeping. If we are not careful, a lot of

our time can be wasted on things which may not be sinful, but they take the place of things which would be more spiritually profitable. We read in Ephesians 5:16, that we must redeem our time, that is 'Make good use of every opportunity you have, because these are evil days'.

Time that is spent in prayer and Bible study, or witnessing for the Lord Jesus, is the most effective in enabling us to produce fruit. Of course we cannot spend all our time doing these things. We have to do business, housework, looking after children, planting and harvesting, tending to animals, and many other duties. Things like reading, hobbies, recreation, etc, have their place to refresh mind and body, but the spare time we have from essential things is very important. Too much time can be spent talking with our friends, or doing things we like to do.

Sometimes we can spend so much time on these secular things that we do not have enough time to pray and study our Bible. Or if we try to squeeze some time in for prayer, our minds are too tired and occupied with what we have been doing, to concentrate in prayer. Bible study is then neglected, and we do not have enough time to go to those who do not know Jesus, to witness for Him.

That is why our time needs to be pruned. Our Heavenly Father as the Gardener, knows what to cut off to make us more fruitful. Sometimes He wants to cut off the things on which we are spending too much time, so that we can give extra time to things which will produce more fruit of the Spirit.

A minister in China asked one of his elders to go with him to a hilly part of the country for four weeks so that they could preach in the villages there. The elder refused, saying that it was the time to plant his rice. But later he was convicted by the Holy Spirit for putting his own work before the work of the Lord. He went with the minister, although the men in the village who were not Christians laughed at him saying, 'You will be begging food from us at harvest time'. When he came back to his village the rice plants of his neighbours were already well above ground. After he planted his rice, there was no rain for some time, and much of the neighbours' rice died. When the rain returned, the elder's rice grew and he had the best harvest in the whole area. He was the one who was able to supply the others with rice that year. Jesus said, 'Be concerned above everything else with the Kingdom of God and with what he requires of you and he will provide you with all these other things' (Matthew 6:33).

Plans

We like to make plans and decide what we want to do. Very often these plans are good but they may not be what God wants. Perhaps it is a plan for our career, or our marriage, or to make some purchase, or to go somewhere. When we pray about it, it is possible that God will impress on us that He has another plan which will enable us to bear more spiritual fruit for Him. 'My thoughts,' says the Lord, 'are not like yours, and my ways are different from yours' (Isaiah 55:8). That is why He sometimes has to prune off some of our ways and our plans.

Very often young Christians make a wrong plan for

their marriage. They go by their own ideas and do not seek God's guidance, or they do not welcome His knife when He wants to cut off that plan! When they get married, their life is not a happy one. Spiritual fruit is hindered. A person may be spending too much time with someone of the opposite sex, which is leading into temptation. Under such circumstances, a Christian will find the Heavenly Gardener coming with His pruning knife to cut off that time. We must let the Heavenly Gardener prune and train our lives, so that we can bear more fruit.

Money

When we become Christians, we must look on our money and possessions in a different way from a worldly person. As children of God we are stewards of all the things he has given us. We are to look after them for Him! It is wrong to use them without consulting Him. He has loaned them to us so that we can use them for His Glory, and to enable us to bear more fruit for Him. If we make plans to use our money just the way we like, it grieves the Holy Spirit. Paul wrote in 2 Corinthians 9:7, 'Each one should give, then, as he has decided, not with regret or out of a sense of duty; for God loves the one who gives gladly'.

Money given to God is like seed - it grows. Jesus said, 'Give to others, and God will give to you. Indeed, you will receive a full measure, a generous helping, poured into your hands - all that you can hold. The measure you use for others, is the one that God will use for you' (Luke 6:38). The Lord does that, not that we will store up a lot for ourselves, but so that we will have more to use for

Him. Let me illustrate this from something my wife and I experienced. We were transferred from one mission station to another, 400 miles away. We sold the house we were leaving, hoping to buy another in the new area. We found that a house in that area would cost quite a lot more than the one we sold.

As we prayed for the extra money, the Lord seemed to be impressing on us that we should give another missionary some of the money we had received from the first house. We thought that was strange. We were asking the Lord for more money, and He was asking us to give away some that we had! When we were sure that the Lord wanted us to do that, we went to the post office to post the letter giving away £400. After posting the letter, we collected our mail from the post office. One of the letters we received was from a person 5000 miles away. In the letter he wrote that he had £2,500 he wanted to send to us - just the extra amount we needed to buy the new house.

To be a fruitful branch then, we must allow God to use His pruning knife, although we may not understand why. He prunes in love, and only takes away the thing that He knows would keep us from being as fruitful as we should be. John Bunyan said, 'I shovel out to God, and He shovels back to me, but His shovel is bigger than mine'. But what God shovels back to us He expects us to use for His glory, so that we will bear more fruit for Him.

Questions

1. Cleansing takes away bad things from us; what does pruning do?

2. Why does the Lord ask us to give up some good things?

3. Why does an athlete not use heavy boots and overcoat when running?

4. Discuss some of the ways a Christian can waste time.

5. Name one or two plans which God may want to prune.

6. With what does the Bible say we must not fall in love?

7. Explain what it means to be God's steward.

8. What is the correct way to use our money and possessions?

9. Discuss what Jesus meant in Luke 6:38.

10. How should we welcome the Lord's pruning of our money and anything else that hinders us?

STUDY EIGHT

THE BRANCH MUST ABIDE IN CHRIST

Reading: Romans 12:1-8

So then, my brothers, because of God's great mercy to us I appeal to you: Offer yourselves as a living sacrifice to God, dedicated to his service and pleasing to him. This is the true worship that you should offer. [2]Do not conform yourselves to the standards of this world, but let God transform you inwardly by a complete change of your mind. Then you will be able to know the will of God - what is good and is pleasing to him and is perfect.

[3]And because of God's gracious gift to me I say to every one of you: Do not think of yourself more highly than you should. Instead, be modest in your thinking, and judge yourself according to the amount of faith that God has given you. [4]We have many parts in the one body, and all these parts have different functions. [5]In the same way, though we are many, we are one body in union with Christ, and we are all joined to each other as different parts of one body. [6]So we are to use our different gifts in accordance with the grace that God has given us. If our gift is to speak God's message, we should do it according to the faith that we have; [7]if it is to serve, we should serve; if it is to teach, we should teach; [8]if it is to encourage others, we should do so. Whoever shares with others should do it generously; whoever has authority should work hard; whoever shows kindness to others should do it cheerfully.

We have studied that one must be born again, spiritually, to become a branch in the Lord Jesus, who is the spiritual Vine. We will see in this study that to abide in Christ means giving ourselves completely to Him. We read this in Romans 12:1, 2, 'Because of God's great mercy to us I appeal to you: offer yourselves as a living sacrifice to God, dedicated to his service and pleasing to him... Do not conform yourselves to the standards of this world, but let God transform you inwardly, by a complete change of your mind. Then you will be able to know the will of God - what is good and is pleasing to Him and is perfect'.

Let us look at what it means to 'offer ourselves as a living sacrifice'. In the Old Testament, dead animals were offered to God as a sacrifice. Now He does not want dead animals - they were only acceptable to Him as a sign that one day Jesus would shed His blood for us. He wants a living sacrifice - a living body in which the Holy Spirit can live and do His work.

We must offer our wills

Our will is the part of us that makes decisions. It is very important that it comes under the control of the Holy Spirit. To be a fruitful branch we must yield our wills to God. We must deny ourselves, by giving up the things we want to do, if they are not pleasing to God. We must be willing to choose to do the things He wants us to do.

You will remember that Jesus set us an example of yielding His will to His Father. He prayed, 'Not what I want, but what You want' (Matthew 26:39). Paul also made that decision. He had been doing what he wanted to do. That was persecuting the Christians - seeing that they were taken to prison, and even killed. But when He met Jesus on the Damascus Road, he fell down and said to Jesus, 'What shall I do, Lord?' (Acts 22:10). From that time on, Paul was under the control of the Holy Spirit, and in spite of trials, torture, beatings, and many other troubles, his will was submitted to God, and he chose to do what He wanted him to do. The only way we can abide in Christ, and be fruitful, is to say the same thing to the Lord, 'Here is my will, what do You want me to do, Lord?' Then we will make the decisions He wants us to make.

We must offer our minds

God has given each of us a mind. In the language of the Bible we read about giving our 'hearts' to the Lord. That does not mean the part of our body that pumps the blood, but it means the 'heart' of our minds. The part that directs our thoughts and desires. When we offer our minds to God, He fills them with good and pure thoughts, and intentions. How does He do that? He gives us a new mind, as we read in Romans 12:2, 'Let God transform you inwardly by a complete change of your mind. Then you will be able to know the will of God'. In fact, He gives us the 'mind of Christ' to control our thoughts and desires. Paul writes, 'Who knows the mind of the Lord? We, however, have the mind of Christ' (1 Corinthians 2:16).

When our minds are given to God we have wonderful fellowship with Him. We also have united fellowship with other Christians, when we all have the same Christ-like mind. We read in Acts 4:32, 'The group of believers was one in mind and heart'. Members who have a self-centred mind cause discord in the church, through pride, envy, jealousy and ambition for their own selfish desires. If our minds are unclean, or selfish, then the thoughts and desires which pass through them are made unclean and sinful. Let us pray to the Lord, 'Take my mind, cleanse and fill it with the mind of Christ, so that I will have your thoughts and desires'.

We must offer our bodies
God has given each of us a body. When the Lord Jesus was in this world He had a body, but as we read in Acts chapter one, He took that body to heaven when He ascended to His Father. He then sent the Holy Spirit to help the church to spread the good news of salvation. But the Holy Spirit came without a body! He is a Spirit. He now wants our bodies as a house in which to live, so that He can use us to do His work. That is why Paul wrote in Romans 12:1, 'Offer yourselves as a living sacrifice to God'. The King James version of the Bible says, 'Present your bodies a living sacrifice'. That is why He asks for your body and mine.

Paul asked the Christians at Corinth, 'Don't you know that your body is the temple of the Holy Spirit, who lives in you and who was given to you by God?... use your bodies for God's glory' (1 Corinthians 6:19, 20). He had already told them in verse 15, 'You know that your bodies are parts of the Body of Christ. Shall I take a part of Christ's Body and make it part of the body of a prostitute?'

In Romans 6:12, 13 we read, 'Sin must no longer rule in your mortal bodies... nor must you surrender any part

of yourselves to sin to be used for wicked purposes'.
Either we allow the Holy Spirit to use the members of our
bodies, or we control them ourselves. Let us see then how
we can allow the Holy Spirit to use the members of our
bodies, after we have given them to Him?

Our hands

We must say to the Lord, 'I give my hands to you to do
the things you want them to do. I will not use them for
anything I know you do not want them to do'. James
writes in his letter, 'Wash your hands you sinners! Purify
your hearts, you hypocrites!' (4:8). And the King James
version translates Psalm 24:3, 4, 'Who shall ascend into
the hill of the Lord? or who shall stand in His holy place?
He that hath clean hands and a pure heart.'

Our tongues

Our tongues must be set aside for the use of the Holy
Spirit. We should pray, 'Lord, I give my tongue to You
to use for your words. By your help and grace I will not
use it for words that would grieve you'. 1 Peter 3:10
states, 'Whoever wants to enjoy life and wishes to see
good times, must keep from speaking evil and stop
telling lies'. A lot of the trouble in our churches is caused
by tongues that say things they should not say.

Our feet

Isaiah 52:7, in the King James version, tells us, 'How
beautiful upon the mountains are the feet of him that
bringeth good tidings, that publisheth peace'. Jesus walked
around the villages of Palestine when He was in this

world, preaching and healing. The Holy Spirit wants to continue that work. He needs our feet, as well as our tongues, to take His message of salvation to the homes of non-Christians, and to lands where people have not yet heard about the Lord Jesus.

Let us say to the Lord, 'I want You to use my feet. Show me where I should go to carry the good news of your salvation. I will not use my feet to go to places where I would be tempted to sin, because I pray 'Lead me not into temptation'. I will not use my feet to go to places where I could not take the Lord Jesus with me.'

The story is told of a girl who was being taken down a mine to see how coal is mined. She arrived at the mine in a white dress. She asked the guide, 'Am I allowed to go down in a white dress?' 'Yes,' was the answer, 'but you will not be able to come up in a white dress!' The guide knew that she was going down into a place that was filled with black dust, so her dress would not remain white. That is what happens if we go into places that are defiled with the evil things of this world. We come out stained with sin.

If we offer to God our will, our mind and our body, then He will be able to make us a fruitful Christian. Do not let us keep any of these from being used by the Holy Spirit.

Questions

1. Describe again how we are grafted into Jesus, the Vine.

2. How can we discover that the will of God is good, pleasing and perfect?

3. What part must our wills serve in abiding in Jesus?

4. What is the usual meaning of the word 'heart' in the Bible?

5. Why does Paul instruct us to present our bodies to God?

6. Discuss the question: How can we use our bodies for God's glory?

7. What do you think the Psalmist means when he refers to 'clean hands' in Psalm 24?

8. Why are our tongues so important to God?

9. What use of the tongue would grieve the Holy Spirit?

10. What type of places defile the Christian?

STUDY NINE

THE HOLY SPIRIT PRODUCES LOVE

Reading: 1 Corinthians 13

I may be able to speak the languages of men and even of angels, but if I have no love, my speech is no more than a noisy gong or a clanging bell. [2]I may have the gift of inspired preaching; I may have all knowledge and understand all secrets; I may have all the faith needed to move mountains - but if I have no love, I am nothing. [3]I may give away everything I have, and even give up my body to be burnt - but if I have no love, this does me no good.

[4]Love is patient and kind; it is not jealous or conceited or proud; [5]love is not ill-mannered or selfish or irritable; love does not keep a record of wrongs; [6]love is not happy with evil, but is happy with the truth. [7]Love never gives up; and its faith, hope, and patience never fail.

[8]Love is eternal. There are inspired messages, but they are temporary; there are gifts of speaking in strange tongues, but they will cease; there is knowledge, but it will pass. [9]For our gifts of knowledge and of inspired messages are only partial; [10]but when what is perfect comes, then what is partial will disappear.

[11]When I was a child, my speech, feelings, and thinking were all those of a child; now that I am a man, I have no more use for childish ways. [12]What we see now is like a dim image in a mirror; then we shall see

face to face. What I know now is only partial; then it
will be complete - as complete as God's knowledge of
me.

[13]Meanwhile these three remain: faith, hope and
love; and the greatest of these is love.

In our last study we found that it is necessary to give
ourselves completely to God. Our wills, our minds, and
our bodies should be offered to Him. It is only then that
He can use us as a fruitful branch in Jesus.

When a branch remains in the vine, the sap flows from
the vine into the branch. It is the sap from the vine that
produces the fruit on the branch, as we have seen in a
previous study. Jesus is the Vine and we are the branches,
we are told in John 15:5. The Holy Spirit flows from
Jesus into us, as sap flows into the branch. If the Holy
Spirit does not flow through us we will not bear fruit,
because Jesus said in the same verse, 'You can do nothing
without me'. Of course we can do things without Jesus,
but those things will not bear spiritual fruit.

In our next few studies we will discuss how the
FRUIT OF THE SPIRIT operates in our lives. You will
remember that Paul wrote in Galatians 5:22, 23, 'The
Spirit produces love, joy, peace, patience, kindness,
goodness, faithfulness, humility, and self-control'. In
this study, let us think of the first part of the fruit - LOVE.

Love for God
First of all, we must remember that GOD IS LOVE (1
John 4:8). When He sends the Holy spirit into our lives,
He fills our hearts with love. Romans 5:5 tell us, 'God has

poured out his love into our hearts by means of the Holy
Spirit who is God's gift to us'. His Holy Spirit produces
much love for God in our hearts. His love helps us to fulfil
the command of Scripture, 'Love the Lord your God with
all your heart, with all your soul, with all your mind and
with all your strength' (Mark 12:30). We can only do that
when we offer our wills, minds and bodies for the use of
the Holy Spirit, as we studied in our last lesson.

That means that we will love to worship God. When
we love someone, we like to spend time with that person.
When we love God we want to spend time alone with
Him in prayer. We want to hear Him speaking to us
through His Word. It gives us much joy, then, to spend
time reading and studying the Bible. We also love to
worship Him in fellowship with other Christians in the
church.

When we love someone, we like to do special things
for that person. When we love God, we want to serve
Him. We love to spend time doing His work. We want to
tell others about Him, and we love to give time and
money to help to spread the good news about Him. If
people do not give willingly to God, of their time and
possessions, it is a very, very bad sign. It shows that they
love themselves more than they love God. They want to
spend most of their time, talents and money on things for
themselves. Paul tells us, 'God loves the one who gives
gladly' (2 Corinthians 9:7).

Love for our neighbour
In Mark 12:31 we are commanded, 'Love your neighbour
as you love yourself'. It is not natural for a person to do

that. It is natural for us to love ourselves much more than we love others, especially if they do things that we do not like! But if we are born again and the love of God is shed abroad in our hearts, then we can love others as we love ourselves. Not in our own strength, but God loves them through us. We love them with God's love!

This was seen one day in court. A prostitute was being tried and sentenced to a term in prison. In the court there was a Christian lady, Miss Booth. She felt the love of God in her heart for the woman who had sinned. She jumped up, rushed to the front of the court, and although the woman was in a very filthy state, she gave her a kiss. The love that the Christian lady had for the prostitute was so strong, she decided to go to prison to see her. When she went to the prison and asked to speak to the prisoner, the person in charge said, 'That woman is mentally disturbed. She walks up and down in the cell all day saying, "Who kissed me?" '

The Christian lady said, 'I am the one who kissed her,' and she was given permission to go to the cell to talk to the prisoner. When she told her that she was the one who kissed her, the prisoner calmed down and listened to the story of how Jesus loved her. As a result, she became a Christian, and when released from prison, she became a worker for the church among women who were still living the life in which she had once engaged.

When the love of God is in our hearts we will pray for others, and want to do all we can to help them to find the Lord Jesus as their Saviour. We will show our concern with kind deeds, because we love them. We do not do that because we expect kindness in return. Jesus said, 'When you give a feast, invite the poor, the crippled, the lame, and the blind; and you will be blessed, because they are not able to pay you back. God will repay you on the day the good people rise from death' (Luke 14:13, 14).

Questions

1. How is spiritual fruit formed in our lives?

2. Is 'love' a separate fruit of the Holy Spirit?

3. Discuss what Paul means in Romans 5:5, when he writes that 'God has poured out His love into our hearts'?

4. How can we love God, 'with all our heart, soul, mind and strength'?

5. Why does a committed Christian love to spend time with God in worship and prayer?

6. If a person does not enjoy spending time in prayer and Bible Study, what conclusion can we reach?

7. Explain how Christians can love people they do not like.

8. Try to imagine how the prostitute felt when Miss Booth jumped up and kissed her.

9. What caused Miss Booth to follow her to prison?

10. In what other way should we show God's love to others, as well as using our tongue?

STUDY TEN

THE HOLY SPIRIT BRINGS JOY

Reading: Psalm 100

Sing to the Lord, all the world!
²Worship the Lord with joy;
come before him with happy songs!

³Acknowledge that the Lord is God.
He made us, and we belong to him;
we are his people, we are his flock.

⁴Enter the temple gates with thanksgiving,
go into its courts with praise.
Give thanks to him and praise him.

⁵The Lord is good;
his love is eternal
and his faithfulness lasts for ever.

Now let us look at the second part of the fruit of the Spirit which Paul mentions in Galatians 5:22 - JOY! As we have already seen, the fruit of the Spirit is made up of different parts, and *joy* is an important part. A fruitful Christian must have *joy*. But many church members do not have joy. Why? It is because they have not fully surrendered their minds, wills and bodies to the control of the Holy Spirit. The Holy Spirit is not flowing through them. When He has full control, He brings joy.

One day a church member, with a very sad and miserable face came to a minister after he had preached on the subject of joy. She said, 'I have joy in my heart'. As the minister looked at her face he said, 'You should tell your heart to let your face know about it!'

Both Old and New Testaments emphasize that a child of God should have joy. Here are some of the references: Nehemiah 8:10, 'The joy that the Lord gives you will make you strong'. Psalm 16:11, 'Your presence fills me with joy and brings me pleasure for ever'. Proverbs 17:22, 'Being cheerful keeps you healthy. It is slow death to be gloomy all the time'. John 16:24, 'Ask and you will receive, so that your happiness may be complete'. Philippians 4:4, 'May you always be joyful in your union with the Lord. I say it again: rejoice!' 1 Thessalonians 5:16, 'Be joyful always'. Also, the Bible has many examples of those who experienced joy.

Joy at Creation
In Job 38:6,7, we read, 'Who laid the corner-stone of the world? In the dawn of that day the stars sang together, and the heavenly beings shouted for joy'.

Joy at Jesus' Birth, Resurrection and Ascension
The night Jesus was born, the angel announced to the shepherds, 'I am here with good news for you, which will bring great joy to all the people' (Luke 2:10). We Christians still have the same opportunity of announcing to men and women, the good news that Jesus came to bring great joy!

When the women came to look at the tomb where Jesus had been buried, they found it open and an angel sitting on the stone which had been a door to the tomb. The angel said to them, 'I know you are looking for Jesus... He is not here; He has been raised... Go quickly now, and tell His disciples, "He has been raised from death".' The women then, '...Left the tomb in a hurry, afraid and yet filled with joy' (Matthew 28:5, 6, 8).

After the resurrection, Jesus spent some time with the disciples and then took them out to Bethany. 'As He was blessing them, he departed from them and was taken up into heaven. They worshipped him and went back into Jerusalem, filled with great joy, and spent all their time in the Temple giving thanks to God' (Luke 24:51-53).

Salvation brings joy

Being forgiven and saved from the guilt and power of sin brings joy. There is joy from the assurance that when we are forgiven, we receive eternal life from Christ. Also there is joy because we know that He has gone to prepare a place for us in heaven. Isaiah wrote in chapter 12 and verse 3, 'As fresh water brings joy to the thirsty, so God's people rejoice when he saves them'.

After David had repented of his sin, he prayed, 'Give me again the joy that comes from your salvation... then I will teach sinners your commands' (Psalm 51:12, 13).

Not only is the one who is forgiven filled with joy, but his salvation brings joy to others. Jesus said in Luke 15:7, 'I tell you, there will be more joy in heaven over one sinner who repents than over ninety-nine respectable people who do not need to repent.'

There is also joy on earth when sinners repent. When Philip preached in Samaria and many people repented, we are told, 'There was great joy in that city' (Acts 8:8). Later in the same chapter, when the Ethiopian official repented and was baptised he 'continued on his way, full of joy' (v 39).

The joy of prayer

The Christian who is filled with the Holy Spirit loves to pray. It gives great joy to talk to one's Heavenly Father. Have you noticed the joy with which a young man talks to the girl to whom he is engaged? If he demonstrates such joy because of earthly love, how much more wonderful it is to talk to the One who has loved us with an everlasting love. King David said to the Lord, 'Your presence fills me with joy and brings me pleasure for ever' (Psalm 16:11). Jesus told His disciples, 'Ask and you will receive, so that your happiness may be complete' (John 16:24).

The joy of Bible study

Jeremiah said to the Lord, 'You spoke to me, and I listened to every word. I belong to you... so your words filled my heart with joy and happiness' (Jeremiah 15:16). Jesus told His Father that He had given His words to the disciples 'so that they might have my joy in their hearts in all its fullness' (John 17:13).

If a young lady receives a letter from one who loves her, or a wife receives a letter from her husband who is away from home, they read the letters with great excitement! When there is true love, they read the letter over and over again, with great pleasure and enjoyment. The Bible contains love letters from God, and the Lord Jesus, to us. We should find great joy in reading their words of love to us.

If a wife received a letter from her husband and she left it lying for many days without opening it, would it not be a sign that her love for him had grown cold? So if God's Word lies unopened in a home, does it not show that love for the Lord is missing? One day a young boy who was playing with a ball in the lounge of his home, found that it had landed on a shelf. When he climbed up to get it he saw a book on the shelf, covered with dust. It was a Bible! He called to his mother, asking her if she knew about the book. 'Yes, she said, it is God's book.' 'Don't you think we should send it back to Him,' the boy said, 'because we never use it'.

The joy of obeying the Lord
In John 15, after Jesus had explained how to remain in Him, he said, 'I have told you this so that my joy may be in you and that your joy may be complete' (v 11). We cannot have joy in prayer, or Bible study, unless we are willing to be obedient to the instructions which Jesus gives to us. A child who is disobedient to its parents, is not a happy child, so a person who is disobedient to God's Word does not have joy. King David said, 'How I love to do your will, my God! I keep your teaching in my heart' (Psalm 40:8).

Joy in difficulties

Although the Bible has many promises of joy for the
Christian, that does not mean that we will be free from all
trials and difficulties. No! but the Bible tells us that 'The
joy that the Lord gives you will make you strong'
(Nehemiah 8:10), so that we can overcome the trials and
tests. Satan has many ways to attack us. Sometimes he
uses people to try us. But Jesus said, 'Happy are you
when people insult you and persecute you and tell all
kinds of evil lies against you because you are my followers. Be happy and glad, for a great reward is kept for you
in heaven' (Matthew 5:11, 12).

Peter warns that we must not be surprised when evil
tests come to us. 'Do not be surprised at the painful test
you are suffering... Rather be glad that you are sharing
Christ's sufferings, so that you may be full of joy when
His glory is revealed' (1 Peter 4:12, 13). Let us then allow
the Holy Spirit to fill us with joy, so that we can bear more
fruit for Him, as joy is part of the fruit of the Spirit,
Galatians 5:22.

Questions

1. Why is it wrong for a Christian to show a sad, miserable attitude?

2. Discuss the reason why more people are not attracted to Jesus?

3. Why is it easier for a joyful Christian to overcome Satan?

4. What kind of news did the angel bring to the shepherds at Jesus' birth?

5. Why were the women at the tomb filled with fear and joy, at the same time?

6. Can you name at least three things that bring joy when we are born again?

7. For what did David pray in Psalm 51, so that he could teach sinners?

8. How do the angels act when a person accepts Jesus as their Saviour?

9. In John 15, Jesus said that if we obey Him we will have two kinds of joy. What are they?

10. Should we let trials and difficulties rob us of our joy?

STUDY ELEVEN

THE HOLY SPIRIT BRINGS PEACE

Reading: John 14:25-31

'I have told you this while I am still with you. [26]The Helper, the Holy Spirit, whom the Father will send in my name, will teach you everything and make you remember all that I have told you.

[27]'Peace is what I leave with you; it is my own peace that I give you. I do not give it as the world does. Do not be worried and upset; do not be afraid. [28]You heard me say to you, "I am leaving, but I will come back to you." If you loved me, you would be glad that I am going to the Father; for he is greater than I. [29]I have told you this now before it all happens, so that when it does happen, you will believe. [30]I cannot talk with you much longer, because the ruler of this world is coming. He has no power over me, [31]but the world must know that I love the Father; that is why I do everything as he commands me.

'Come, let us go from this place.'

We now discuss the third part of the fruit of the Spirit in the life of a Christian. In our reading we saw how Jesus planned that His followers should have His PEACE in their hearts.

What is peace?

When two nations, or tribes, have been engaged in war, and the fighting comes to an end, we say there is peace. The word 'peace' in the Old Testament is 'shalom', which means, 'everything is in order', or 'everything is all right'. Peace then, as part of the fruit of the Spirit, means that all is well in our spiritual lives. Instead of anxiety and turmoil in our minds, the Holy Spirit brings rest and confidence that the Lord is working all things out for us according to His will. As we will see later in the study, that is because we have peace with God.

The wicked have no peace

A person who is not a real Christian does not have peace. The sinful things one does upsets one's conscience and mind. A war goes on in the mind. In Isaiah 57:20, 21, the Lord says, 'Evil men are like the restless sea, whose waves never stop rolling in, bringing filth and muck. There is no safety (peace, KJV) for sinners, says the Lord.' Sinful things are likened to filth and muck being constantly cast up into the mind of the person who is guilty. There is a war going on in their minds, although they may try to hide it.

The Christian has peace

When a person comes to the Lord in true repentance and sorrow for all the wrong things he or she has done, the Bible promises that God will forgive. Not only is there forgiveness, but there is cleansing from the guilt and stains of sin. 1 John 1:9 describes what happens, 'If we confess our sins to God, he will keep his promise and do what is right: he will forgive us our sins and purify us from all our wrongdoing'.

When a person continues in sin, he or she is fighting a war with God, who hates sinful things. But Jesus came to bring peace between the sinner and God. When Christ was born, the angels sang, 'Peace on earth to those with whom he is pleased!' (Luke 2:14). That is why it is possible for us to have peace with God.

Peace with God

The peace which Jesus brings to a Christian is 'peace with God'. Paul wrote in Romans 5:1, 'Now that we have been put right with God through faith, we have peace with God through our Lord Jesus Christ'. How does Jesus bring to us 'peace with God'? Before we repent and surrender to Christ, as our Saviour and Lord, we are following Satan, and Satan is at war with God. Satan leads people to rebel against God, as he led Adam and Eve to do in the garden of Eden. He said to them, 'Did God really tell you not to eat fruit from any tree in the garden? ... When you eat it you will be like God and know what is good and what is bad' (Genesis 3:1, 4). They believed him and rebelled against God. From that time everyone born into this world has a sinful and rebellious spirit. That is why David prayed, 'I have been evil from the day I was born; from the time I was conceived, I have been sinful' (Psalm 51:5).

A person who is not a Christian is serving God's enemy, and by doing sinful things is fighting against God. But when we invite Jesus into our lives as our Saviour and Lord, He forgives us for our sin and rebellion against God. He is able to do that because He took our punishment for us when He died on the cross, as Isaiah 53:5,6, tells us, 'Because of our sins he was wounded... the Lord made the punishment fall on him, the punishment all of us deserved'. That is why He is able to reconcile us to God, as Paul writes in Romans 5:10, 'We were God's enemies, but he made us his friends through the death of his Son'. That is how we can have peace with God.

Peace with others

We read in Hebrews 12:14, 'Try to be at peace with everyone', and in Romans 12:18, 'Do everything possible on your part to live in peace with everybody'. Then Paul instructs us in Romans 14:19, 'We must always aim at those things that bring peace and that help to strengthen one another'. Jesus wants peace in His Body, the Church, so that it can work well. If the members of our bodies did not work well together we would be in trouble. Our left hand does not get jealous of our right hand because we always use it to shake hands! Our ears do not get jealous of our nose because it has a more prominent position! When we are in good health all our body's members work peacefully together. That is how we are able to control our bodies so that it can fulfil all its functions. It is only when Christians live together peacefully in the Body of Christ that He can use the Church for His glory.

If church members quarrel with one another, the peace in the church is broken. If they gossip about one another it causes turmoil. To keep the peace of the Holy Spirit in our church fellowships, we must be open with one another. If there is any misunderstanding between us and another Christian, we must go directly to that Christian and talk over the matter, as Jesus instructs us to do, 'Do it privately, just between yourselves' (Matthew 18:15).

Peace is like a referee

When a game is being played, there is a referee, or umpire, to control the game and see that the rules of the game are followed and that there is no foul play. With a whistle, or a shout, the players are stopped when the rules are broken. In our Christian lives, peace is like a referee. It guides us in understanding what the Lord wants us to do. It warns us when we are being tempted to do something that would grieve the Holy Spirit.

Paul explains this when he writes, 'God's peace, which is far beyond human understanding, will keep your hearts and minds safe in union with Christ Jesus' (Philippians 4:7).

Let us end this study with words from the Lord Jesus Christ and Paul, showing the importance of peace as a part of the fruit of the Spirit in our lives. Jesus said to His disciples, 'Peace is what I leave with you; it is my own peace that I give you' (John 14:27). 'May the Lord himself, who is our source of peace, give you peace at all times and in every way,' Paul writes in 2 Thessalonians 3:16.

Questions

1. What brings the peace of God into our lives?

2. Why do sinners not experience peace in their minds?

3. Describe the war that goes on inside people who have not made peace with God.

4. How can that war end, and peace be declared?

5. The angel promised 'Peace on earth to...' Can you complete the sentence?

6. Discuss how Jesus can declare peace in our lives.

7. What does it mean to be reconciled to God?

8. What disturbs peace in our churches?

9. Can you give the reference of the text which tells us to: 'Try to be at peace with everyone'? And what does it mean?

10. Describe how peace is like a referee or umpire?

STUDY TWELVE

THE HOLY SPIRIT BRINGS PATIENCE

Reading: Romans 15:4-7

Everything written in the Scriptures was written to teach us, in order that we might have hope through the patience and encouragement which the Scriptures give us. [5]And may God, the source of patience and encouragement, enable you to have the same point of view among yourselves by following the example of Christ Jesus, [6]so that all of you together may praise with one voice the God and Father of our Lord Jesus Christ.

[7]Accept one another, then, for the glory of God, as Christ has accepted you.

Another part of the fruit of the Spirit is PATIENCE. Very often in the life of Christians, it is the lack of patience that spoils the rest of the fruit. It specially disturbs the peace which we discussed in our last study. We have all seen fruit which looks alright on the outside, but when we prepare to eat it we find there is a bad part inside. That bad part spoils the fruit. Impatience does that with the fruit of the Spirit.

God has been patient with us

Paul wrote to Timothy, 'God was merciful to me in order that Christ Jesus might show his full patience in dealing with me, the worst of sinners' (1 Timothy 1:16). We have all wandered and gone astray like sheep, but God was patient with us, and sent Jesus to take the punishment that we deserved, as Isaiah tells us in chapter 53. And in Romans 3:23, we are reminded that we have all sinned, but God patiently waited for us to repent. Jesus told the story of the prodigal son in Luke 15, to show us how God waits patiently for the return of the sinner as the father waited for his son to return.

Those of us who have repented and are now God's children know how much patience He still has to have with us. He patiently teaches us the way we should live the Christian life, and how we can become more like Christ. Some of us are slow to learn, but He is very patient with us.

We must wait patiently for God

We read in Psalm 37:7, 'Be patient and wait for the Lord to act'. Sometimes our prayers are not answered as quickly as we would like, and at other times they are not answered the way we would like them to be answered. At these times we can be tempted to be impatient with God. That disturbs our peace with Him, and worry takes its place. David warns about this danger in Psalm 27:14, 'Trust in the Lord. Have faith, do not despair'. That is why he could write in Psalm 40:1, 'I waited patiently for the Lord's help'. If we are impatient with God, it means that we are blaming Him for not being able to cope.

We must be patient with others

Paul wrote to the church in Ephesus, 'Be always humble, gentle, and patient. Show your love by being tolerant with one another' (Ephesians 4:2). Jesus told the story of a king who forgave a man a very large debt. When the forgiven man met a person who owed him a small sum of money, he demanded his money right away. He was asked to have patience and it would be paid, but the man who had been forgiven so much had no patience to wait for him to pay. He had him sent to prison. When the king heard what had happened, he withdrew his forgiveness and had the first man put in prison. Then Jesus went on to say, 'That is how my Father in heaven will treat every one of you unless you forgive your brother from your heart' (Matthew 18:22-35).

God has been very patient with us, who are Christians, as we have seen. He has forgiven us for many things, so now we must be patient with others. If we are not willing to forgive, then we are asking God to forgive us in the same way, because we pray in the Lord's prayer, 'Forgive us our wrongs as we forgive those who wrong us' (Matthew 6:12). In Colossians 3:13, we are told, 'Be tolerant with one another and forgive one another whenever any of you has a complaint against someone else.' In the above reading in Matthew, Peter asked Jesus if it would be all right to only forgive seven times, if some one does wrong to you. Jesus said he should be forgiven 490 times, meaning that there should be no limit.

We must be patient when trials come

Because patience is such an important part of the fruit of the Spirit, James tells us, 'Let patience have her perfect work' (James 1:4 [KJV]). How does patience work? If we never had any trials or difficulties we would not need patience, so it means that patience works hardest when we are having problems! Romans 5:3 (KJV) states, 'We glory in tribulations... knowing that tribulation works patience'. Then in Romans 12:12, 'Let your hope keep you joyful, be patient in your troubles, and pray at all times'.

James also writes in his letter, 'My brothers, remember the prophets who spoke in the name of the Lord. Take them as examples of patient endurance under suffering... You have heard of Job's patience, and you know how the Lord provided for him in the end' (James 5:10, 11). We will all have temptations to be impatient - Satan will see to that! People will do things which will try our patience.

Things which we want may not be given to us. Plans which we make, may not work out the way we would like them to do. Illness may come. We may be misjudged. When these things happen, our patience is tried, but as we have read in the above verses, these trials should make our patience grow. And as patience is part of the fruit of the Spirit, it becomes a witness to others. The Lord, through the Holy Spirit, provides the grace to enable our patience to grow under these difficulties. That is why we are told, 'Let us run with patience the race that is set before us' (Hebrews 12:1 [KJV]).

To sum up then: God has much patience with us, so we must wait patiently for Him to work out His will in our lives. We must be patient with others, and we must allow patience to grow in our lives when we face the difficulties and trials which come to us as we fight the good fight of faith.

Questions

1. Compare God's patience with sinners, as illustrated by the father of the prodigal son.

2. How does impatience hinder us from bearing spiritual fruit?

3. What did David mean when he said he had patiently waited for God?

4. How does Paul advise that Christians should treat one another?

5. What did he mean when he tells us to be tolerant with one another?

6. When is our patience tried most severely?

7. How should we act when we are patiently waiting for solutions to our problems?

8. Where are we to look for examples of patience according to James?

9. Name one or two things which try our patience.

10. What effect does our patience have on others who see us practising it in trials and difficulties?

STUDY THIRTEEN

THE HOLY SPIRIT BRINGS KINDNESS

Reading Ephesians 4:29-32

Do not use harmful words, but only helpful words, the kind that build up and provide what is needed, so that what you say will do good to those who hear you. [30] And do not make God's Holy Spirit sad; for the Spirit is God's mark of ownership on you, a guarantee that the Day will come when God will set you free. [31] Get rid of all bitterness, passion, and anger. No more shouting or insults, no more hateful feelings of any sort. [32] Instead, be kind and tender-hearted to one another, and forgive one another, as God has forgiven you through Christ.

In this study we will look at KINDNESS as part of the fruit of the Holy Spirit - not just human kindness. Naturally we are kind to those people we love, but the kindness which the Holy Spirit brings to us causes us to be kind even to those who are our enemies. As we saw in Study Nine, the Holy Spirit brings the love of God into our hearts. It is the love of God in our hearts that gives us the desire to be kind to everyone.

Kindness is part of God's nature

Paul explains the kindness of God in Ephesians 2:6, 7, '(God) hath raised us up together, and made us sit together in heavenly places in Christ Jesus: that in the ages to come he might show the exceeding riches of his grace in his kindness toward us through Christ Jesus' (KJV). While all were sinners, God sent the Lord Jesus to die for us, so that we could be forgiven and go to heaven to live with Him. What wonderful kindness to sinners, kindness which we do not deserve.

We must be kind to others

Paul then goes on to tell us that if God has been so kind to us, we must show that kindness to others. We read in verse 32 of the reading at the top of this study, 'Be kind and tender-hearted to one another, and forgive one another, as God has forgiven you through Christ'. In the previous verse he tells us to, 'Get rid of all bitterness, passion and anger. No more shouting or insults, no more hateful feelings of any sort.' It is only the love of God shed abroad in our hearts by the Holy Spirit, as we read in Romans 5:5, that rids our hearts of these unkind things.

Kindness in the home

The first place we must practise the kindness of the Holy Spirit is in the home. 'Husbands, love your wives and do not be harsh with them,' we read in Colossians 3:19. One day a headmaster called me into his home. He admitted that he had a very short temper, and when his wife did something he did not like he would strike her. He asked for prayer, but I told him, 'You need more than prayer, you need to be born again, as Jesus told Nicodemus, so that the Holy Spirit will live in your heart and replace the anger with kindness.' He repented, prayed, and asked the Lord Jesus into his life. He became a new man in Christ, and at the time of writing he is a very successful minister of the church. Many husbands are unkind to their wives and it destroys peace in the home.

Sometimes wives are also unkind to their husbands. In Proverbs 21:19, we are told, 'Better to live out in the desert than with a nagging, complaining wife'. But the writer also describes a kind wife, 'In her tongue is the law of kindness... Her children arise up, and call her blessed; her husband also, and he praiseth her' (Proverbs 31:26, 28 [KJV]). Children who grow up in a home where mother and father show the kindness of the Holy Spirit to one another and to them, see a wonderful example of the type of home they should have when they are married.

Kindness to our enemies

A person who is not a Christian is naturally angry with anyone who does wrong to him. When a person has the fruit of the Holy Spirit in his life, the Holy Spirit produces kindness to enemies. Paul, quoting from the Proverbs, told the Christians in the church in Rome, 'If your enemy is hungry, feed him; if he is thirsty, give him a drink; for by doing this you will make him burn with shame' (Romans 12:20). Showing kindness melts hatred!

Stephen when he was being stoned to death, showed kindness to his murderers. He prayed, 'Lord! Do not remember this sin against them!' (Acts 7:60). David showed great kindness to the grandson of his old enemy, Saul. He took the young man into his palace and treated him like a son (2 Samuel 9).

Practical ways of showing kindness

First of all, our kindness should spring out of our love for the Lord. What we do for others should be done for His sake, because He has been so kind to us. Jesus said that He will say at the end of the world to those who practised kindness in His name, 'Whenever you did this for one of the least important of these brothers of mine, you did it for Me!' (Matthew 25:40).

We should be kind to our church and its leaders, because it is Christ's bride! We should not only give cheerfully of our money as the Lord prospers us, but we should find ways of servicing our church. There are opportunities for cleaning, gardening, repairing, painting etc, in many cases. In these ways we can show kindness to the house of God, because sometimes buildings and grounds are left in a way that is a disgrace to the bride of Christ. Then there are opportunities for teaching in Sunday School, youth work, visiting the sick, bringing others to services. These are some of the spiritual activities that need to be done.

Then there are many opportunities of showing kindness in the home. We can volunteer to help one another with jobs that have to be done. We can express thanks when things are done for us, instead of taking them for granted. Also in the office, factory, farm or shop where we work, there are many opportunities to show kindness to fellow-workers. By taking an interest in the welfare of their families, and going out of our way to assist them in any problems they have, will allow us to practise the fruit of the Spirit in the kindness we show.

We can visit those who are ill, or send a letter, or card,

if they are not near. If they are near, ladies could do some jobs for them, like cooking meals, looking after the children for a time, or shopping. Men can help with repairs in the homes of the elderly, doing jobs like cutting the lawn, gardening etc. If there has been a bereavement, a prayer in the home can mean so much to the bereaved. In fact, prayer for any problem in the life, or home, of a person well known to us, is usually appreciated, as are words of encouragement for those who are depressed or discouraged.

Jesus said that even a cup of cold water will not lose its reward if given in the name of a disciple, but He pointed out that we must not boast about any kindness we show. He said in Matthew 6:1, 'Make sure you do not perform your religious duties in public so that people will see what you do. If you do these things publicly, you will not have any reward from your Father in heaven.' The kindness which the fruit of the Holy Spirit produces in us, does not want to boast, or bring glory to ourselves, but wants all the glory to go to God, Who has given us His Holy Spirit.

Questions

1. What is the difference between human kindness and the kindness which is part of the fruit of the Spirit?

2. Describe God's kindness to sinners.

3. What happens in a home where unkindness is shown by husband or wife?

4. What impression remains with children who are brought up in a home where unkindness is practised?

5. What does Paul tell us we should get rid of in our homes, and churches?

6. How did Stephen show kindness to his murderers?

7. What should be our motive when we show kindness to someone?

8. Describe some ways in which we can be kind to the Church which is Christ's bride?

9. How, then, can we show kindness in the home, workplace, school, etc?

10. Can you think of anyone else to whom you can show kindness?

STUDY FOURTEEN

THE HOLY SPIRIT BRINGS GOODNESS

Reading Ephesians 5:6-11

Do not let anyone deceive you with foolish words; it is because of these very things that God's anger will come upon those who do not obey him. ⁷So have nothing at all to do with such people. ⁸You yourselves used to be in the darkness, but since you have become the Lord's people, you are in the light. So you must live like people who belong to the light, ⁹for it is the light that brings a rich harvest of every kind of goodness, righteousness, and truth. ¹⁰Try to learn what pleases the Lord. ¹¹Have nothing to do with the worthless things that people do, things that belong to the darkness. Instead, bring them out to the light.

In our last study we saw that kindness is an important part of the fruit of the Spirit. Because God is kind, He puts kindness into our hearts through the Holy Spirit. The reason He is kind, is because He is good. He is kind in His actions because He is good in His character. In this study let us look at the GOODNESS of God which He puts into our hearts as part of the fruit of the Holy Spirit. We are told in the above reading, 'Brings a rich harvest of every kind of goodness' (verse 9).

The Lord is good

These are the words of the Psalmist in Psalm 100:5. We know that God is righteous and holy, but an important part of His nature is goodness. It was because of His goodness that He was kind enough to send Jesus to die so that we could be forgiven, Isaiah 53:6. We know from John 3:16 that He loved the people in the world so much that He did not want us to be punished for our sins. He wanted us to have eternal life so that we could live with Him forever in heaven.

The goodness of God causes Him to love sinners, but to hate their sin. Peter tells us, 'He does not want anyone to be destroyed, but wants all to turn away from their sins' (2 Peter 3:9). That is why He listens to us when we come in true repentance and sorrow for sin, asking for forgiveness. He then assures us that our sins will never be held against us any more, Isaiah 43:25; 1 John 1:9. It is His goodness that invites us to come to Him in prayer at any time. We have nothing in ourselves to merit such an invitation.

The goodness of God shown in the life of Jesus

The basic meaning of good, is to be like God, but we have never seen God. However, He sent the Lord Jesus into the world, and Jesus said, 'Whoever has seen me has seen the Father' (John 14:9). We have not seen Jesus, as the disciples saw Him, but they have written and told us what He is like. Their descriptions of Jesus' compassion, love for sinners, willingness to forgive, miraculous power to heal, feeding the hungry, raising the dead, suffering the agony of scourging and death on the cross, and rising victorious out of the tomb, help us to see what a great and good God we have.

The goodness of God then, which is put into our lives as part of the fruit of the Spirit, helps us to become more and more like Jesus. That is how we become more Godly. Paul describes what happens in the life of a Christian. 'All of us, then, reflect the glory of the Lord with uncovered faces; and that same glory, coming from the Lord, who is the Spirit, transforms us into His likeness in an ever greater degree of glory' (2 Corinthians 3:18).

The goodness of God produces Christlike deeds in our lives

In our reading at the beginning of this study we found, 'You must live like people who belong to the light, for it is the light that brings a rich harvest of every kind of goodness, righteousness and truth'. Jesus said, 'A good person brings good out of the treasure of good things in his heart' (Luke 6:45). It is the Holy Spirit who stores goodness in the heart of a Christian, and the Lord must have the praise for any good things we are enabled to do. Jesus also explains this in Matthew 5:16, 'Your light must shine before people, so that they will see the good things you do and praise your Father in heaven'. We are not to receive the praise!

Good must also be done to our enemies

Jesus said, 'Love your enemies, do good to those who hate you, bless those who curse you, and pray for those who ill-treat you' (Luke 6:27). The more like Jesus we become, the more good works we will do, not to gain any

merit, but to express the goodness of the Holy Spirit Who
has been placed in our hearts. Paul explained this to the
Ephesian Christians when he wrote, 'God has made us
what we are, and in our union with Christ Jesus he has
created us for a life of good deeds, which he has already
prepared for us to do' (Ephesians 2:10). God loved us
when we were His enemies, His goodness in our hearts
causes us to love our enemies.

Goodness causes us to hate evil

Romans 12:9, 21 show us that goodness requires hatred
for evil, 'Hate what is evil, hold on to what is good... Do
not let evil defeat you; instead, conquer evil with good'.
Clinging to what is good means holding on when we are
tempted, or discouraged, or depressed, or disappointed.
Hating evil means we must keep as far away from it as we
can. We pray in the Lord's prayer, 'Lead us not into
temptation'. It is foolish to pray that prayer if we walk
into circumstances where we know we will be tempted!
I knew a small boy whose father had a grocery shop. The
boy loved chocolate biscuits, but his father had told him
never to take any from the shop, without asking. The boy
told me that it was very hard to resist the temptation, and
sometimes when his father was not looking, he would
quickly take a biscuit out of the tin. I asked him where he
stood in the shop. 'Right beside the biscuit tin,' he said.
It was no wonder he was tempted! I then tried to show him
how easy it was for Satan to tempt him. We should stay
as far away as possible from all people and things which
tempt us.

Everyone will be tempted

Although it is our responsibility to keep as far away as possible from things which tempt us, temptation will come to us! We will be tempted to think bad thoughts, say wrong words, and do actions which we should not do. Satan will always be hanging around to tempt us. He will want us to read literature, or look at films which would defile our minds. He will try to attract us to unholy places, or the wrong kind of friendships.

Temptations came to the Lord Jesus, and we find that He defeated Satan by quoting God's Word to him. But Adam and Eve, in the garden of Eden, listened to Satan's lies, and decided to do what he wanted them to do. Judas listened to Satan, and decided to betray Jesus. Peter listened to him and denied Jesus. Although these temptations come to us, we have a wonderful promise in the Bible which assures us that we do not need to fall into temptation. Paul writes in 1 Corinthians 10:13, 'Every test that you have experienced is the kind that normally comes to people. But God keeps his promise, and will not allow you to be tested beyond your power to remain firm; at the time you are put to the test, he will give you the strength to endure it, and so provide you with a way out'.

It is the goodness of the Spirit of God in our hearts that causes us to hate evil things. Although the Devil may tempt, or test us with them, the Spirit of God changes us so that we react quickly against Satan.

Questions

1. What is the difference between kindness and goodness?

2. Describe why God loves sinners, but hates sin.

3. How do we receive true goodness into our character?

4. Why must we avoid taking the praise to ourselves for any good we do?

5. How do we reflect more and more God's goodness and glory?

6. What does Paul tell us we should use to overcome evil?

7. What did Jesus teach His disciples to pray, so that they would practise goodness?

8. Is temptation a sin?

9. How can we be sure that temptation will never be too strong for us?

10. Why did a good couple like Adam and Eve fall into temptation?

STUDY FIFTEEN

THE HOLY SPIRIT PRODUCES FAITHFULNESS

Reading: Hebrews 11:32-40

Should I go on? There isn't enough time for me to speak of Gideon, Barak, Samson, Jephthah, David, Samuel, and the prophets. [33]Through faith they fought whole countries and won. They did what was right and received what God had promised. They shut the mouths of lions, [34]put out fierce fires, escaped being killed by the sword. They were weak, but became strong; they were mighty in battle and defeated the armies of foreigners. [35]Through faith women received their dead relatives raised back to life.

Others, refusing to accept freedom, died under torture in order to be raised to a better life. [36]Some were mocked and whipped, and others were put in chains and taken off to prison. [37]They were stoned, they were sawn in two, they were killed by the sword. They went round clothed in skins of sheep or goats - poor, persecuted, and ill-treated. [38]The world was not good enough for them! They wandered like refugees in the deserts and hills, living in caves and holes in the ground.

[39]What a record all of these have won by their faith! Yet they did not receive what God had promised, [40]because God had decided on an even better plan for us. His purpose was that only in company with us would they be made perfect.

The next part of the fruit of the Holy Spirit, mentioned by Paul, is FAITHFULNESS. This word is often used to describe the state that exists between a husband and wife. They are faithful to each other when the husband is not involved with another woman, or the wife with another man. If that should happen we say that the husband or wife has become unfaithful. In many cases we find that wives remain faithful to husbands even when they are cruel! I knew one wife whose husband used to beat her when he found her praying. That existed for over 10 years, but she did not go away from him. Her faithfulness was rewarded because, after 10 years, her husband became a Christian.

Faithfulness in marriage is an illustration of faithfulness in the Christian life, between a person and God. Just as a husband should not have any other woman in place of his wife, so God says, 'Worship no god but me' (Exodus 20:3). Most of us are not tempted to worship gods of wood or stone. But an idol, or god, is anything to which we 'give excessive, or extreme, devotion', according to the dictionary. If we love anything, or anyone, more than we love God, then we are being unfaithful to Him. That is why James writes, 'Unfaithful people! Don't you know that to be the world's friend means to be God's enemy?' In fact the King James version of the Bible calls that spiritual adultery (James 4:4).

God is faithful to us

Paul wrote about the faithfulness of God. 'He who calls you will do it, because he is faithful' (1 Thessalonians 5:24). Again he writes in 1 Corinthians 1:9, 'God is to be trusted, the God who called you to have fellowship with his Son Jesus Christ, our Lord'. This means that He will never be unfaithful to us as some husbands are to their wives. We read in Hebrews 13:5, 'Keep your lives free from the love of money, and be satisfied with what you have. For God has said, "I will never leave you; I will never abandon you".'

We have all been unfaithful to God, because we have all sinned, as Paul reminds us in Romans 3:23. Yet when we come, through Jesus, with true repentance, forsaking our sins, and the things which we have loved more than God, we read, 'If we confess our sins to God, he will keep his promise and do what is right: he will forgive us our sins and purify us from all wrongdoing' (1 John 1:9). Jesus said, 'When I go you will not be left all alone; I will come back to you' (John 14:18).

We must be faithful to God

We have seen that God has promised to be faithful to us through the Lord Jesus Christ, and the Holy Spirit. He will never run away or leave us, but that means that we must be faithful to Him! 1 Corinthians 4:1, 2, makes that clear, 'You should think of us as Christ's servants, who have been put in charge of God's secret truths. The one thing required of such a servant is that he be faithful to his master'.

How can we be faithful in our relationship with God and the Lord Jesus Christ? That is where we need the fruit of the Holy Spirit to work in our hearts. In one of our other studies we saw that love is the first part of the fruit of the Spirit that is mentioned in Galatians 5:22, 23. 'God has poured out His love into our hearts by means of the Holy Spirit, who is God's gift to us', we read in Romans 5:5. Because we love God, we do not want to do anything that would grieve Him and make Him sad, just as a husband who really loves his wife would not be guilty of being unfaithful to her. To be faithful to God, we must say 'NO' to anything, or to any person, that would tempt us to be unfaithful to Him.

Faithfulness to God brings opposition from the world
Worldly people do not like us to be faithful to God, because that means that we are unfaithful to the one they serve, Satan. Very often they oppose us. Satan hates God and does not like anyone to love and serve Him. Satan uses his servants to try to get us to be unfaithful to God. They may laugh at us, or criticise us; they may tell false stories about us; or they may tempt us to join with them in things that would grieve the Lord.

Jesus set us an example of how to be faithful to God when we are opposed or persecuted, as Peter tells us. 'Christ himself suffered for you and left you an example, so that you would follow in his steps. When he was insulted, he did not answer back with an insult; when he suffered he did not threaten, but placed his hopes in God the righteous Judge' (1 Peter 2:21, 23). Jesus remained faithful to His Father, even though He was treated very cruelly by those who did not love God.

Some Christians have had to suffer a great deal to remain faithful to God! In 1953 I was in Kenya during the Mau Mau uprising. I saw many Christians there who suffered for their faith. I stood by the grave of a woman who had died because she refused to deny Jesus. Some men said to her, 'If you do not give up Christianity we are going to kill you'. She answered, 'Jesus is my friend, I cannot run away from Him now'. The men pulled the baby from her back, took her into the bushes and killed her.

I talked with an evangelist whose head had many scars. He told me that he had received a letter from the Mau Mau group in his area, telling him that he must stop preaching about Jesus, or he would be killed. He refused to stop, and one day as he returned from conducting a service in a village school, a gang was waiting for him on a lonely path. With large knives, they chopped his head, and left him lying on the path, thinking he was dead. He was found by some Christians and carried to a Mission Hospital. The doctor told me that he had very little hope for the evangelist's recovery, but he called the African minister and they prayed. Then he operated, and the evangelist made a very speedy recovery. In one month he was able to leave hospital, although his head was still bandaged. The evangelist told me that his friends wanted him to hide when he left hospital, in case he was attacked again, but he said, 'That was Satan trying to frighten me so that I would stop telling people about Jesus'. He went back to his village and continued to preach in the local churches. What wonderful faithfulness to his Saviour.

A minister's wife woke one night and found that the thatch of their manse was on fire. She and her husband ran outside, to find a Mau Mau gang waiting. They had set fire to the thatch. The gang demanded the husband to promise that he would never preach about Jesus again. He said that he could not agree, and was told, 'Then we are going to kill you'. 'If you kill me, I will just go to be with Jesus,' he said. He and his wife were taken into the woods and a rope was tied around his neck. The other end of the rope was thrown over a high branch of a tree, and the minister was pulled up off the ground and left hanging until he was unconscious. Then he was lowered to the ground and cold water thrown over him until he revived. He was asked again if he would stop preaching, and when he told them that his answer was still the same, he was pulled up off the ground again. That was repeated three times! Three times he became unconscious, three times he was revived, and each time his answer was the same. The fourth time the cold water could not revive him, he had gone to be with the One he loved, the Lord Jesus Christ.

His wife had to watch this cruel execution of her husband. When he died she was asked, 'Will you now promise to give up Christianity?' 'No!' she said, 'my answer is the same as my husband's answer, I cannot turn from my Jesus'. 'All right,' they said, 'we are now going to lock you up. It is nearly sunrise and we are afraid of the police finding us, but tonight you will die like your husband.' However, during the day she escaped, and was able to tell what had happened to her husband.

When we see how the above African Christians remained faithful to God, and were willing to die rather than deny Him, it should make many church members today feel very ashamed of being afraid to stand up for Jesus. Jesus said in Mark 8:38, 'If a person is ashamed of me and my teaching in this godless and wicked day, then the Son of Man will be ashamed of him when he comes in the glory of his Father with the Holy angels'. We need the Holy Spirit in our lives to produce that part of His fruit - FAITHFULNESS.

Questions

1. Explain what is meant by faithfulness between a husband and wife.

2. How does a Christian remain faithful to God?

3. Do you remember what James calls falling in love with earthly things?

4. In what verse of Scripture do we read that the Lord will always be faithful to us?

5. What part of the fruit of the Spirit enables us to be faithful to God?

6. Why does Satan try to tempt us to be unfaithful to God?

7. How does Satan try to tempt us to be unfaithful to God?

8. Describe how Jesus acted when He was insulted and tempted?

9. What will be the result, if we are ashamed of Jesus?

10. When was Peter unfaithful to Jesus?

STUDY SIXTEEN

THE HOLY SPIRIT PRODUCES HUMILITY

Reading: Luke 6:27-36

'But I tell you who hear me: Love your enemies, do good to those who hate you, [28]bless those who curse you, and pray for those who ill-treat you. [29]If anyone hits you on one cheek, let him hit the other one too; if someone takes your coat, let him have your shirt as well. [30]Give to everyone who asks you for something, and when someone takes what is yours, do not ask for it back. [31]Do for others just what you want them to do for you.

[32]'If you love only the people who love you, why should you receive a blessing? Even sinners love those who love them! [33]And if you do good only to those who do good to you, why should you receive a blessing? Even sinners do that! [34]And if you lend only to those from whom you hope to get it back, why should you receive a blessing? Even sinners lend to sinners, to get back the same amount! [35]No! Love your enemies and do good to them; lend and expect nothing back. You will then have a great reward, and you will be sons of the Most High God. For he is good to the ungrateful and the wicked. [36]Be merciful just as your Father is merciful.'

We now study another part of the fruit of the Spirit - HUMILITY. In the King James version it is called meekness. Translators have used both humility and meekness to describe the same original word in Greek. Jesus said in the sermon on the mount, 'Happy are those who are humble; they will receive what God has promised!' (Matthew 5:5). The Bible gives us a number of examples of people who were humble, and some examples of those who were proud.

Moses was humble

Moses was very humble. We read in Numbers 12:3, 'Moses was a humble man, more humble than anyone else on earth'. When that was said of him, he was having a lot of trouble with his brother and sister, Aaron and Miriam. It seems that Miriam did not like Moses' wife because her ancestors had come from Africa, and so they criticised Moses and said, 'Has the Lord spoken only through Moses?' It seems pride had crept into their hearts, and they felt they could lead as well as Moses, although God had chosen him.

Moses remained very humble and we do not hear of him getting upset about the criticism. However, God was very displeased with the pride of Aaron and Miriam, and punished them, as we read in the following verses of this chapter in Numbers. But humility, or meekness, is not weakness! When the Children of Israel disobeyed God, Moses showed spiritual strength to challenge them. We read that when Moses came down the mountain with the ten commandments written on stone, he found the people had made a golden calf and were worshipping it. In Exodus 32:19, we are told, 'When Moses came close enough to the camp to see the bull-calf and to see the people dancing, he was furious.' He arranged to have them punished very severely.

A person who has the humility of the Holy Spirit, has two sides then. If he or she is attacked personally with criticism, opposition, or suffering, it is taken humbly, but if the criticism or opposition is an attack on God and His Word, or His work, then the person puts up a spiritual fight, not for himself or herself, but for the honour of the Lord and His cause.

The humility of David

David's son, Absalom, turned against his father and arranged a coup. As David was fleeing for his life, a man called Shimei ran after him shouting insults, cursing him, and accusing him of being a very bad criminal. David's soldiers wanted him to have Shimei killed, but David refused and said, 'Perhaps the Lord will notice my misery and give me some blessing to take the place of his curse'. David could have had him executed immediately, but he took humbly the personal attack, as it was against himself, not the Lord (2 Samuel 16:12).

However, when David found out that someone was defying God, and attacking God's people, like Moses, he became very upset and depended on the Spirit of God to give him the strength to fight for the Lord, and see these people punished. For instance, when he visited his brothers in the army, and saw Goliath defying the Lord, he decided to fight the giant, although his big brothers were afraid and ran from him with the other soldiers. His brothers became jealous of him. But in deciding to attack Goliath, he humbly confessed to Saul, 'The Lord has saved me from lions and bears; he will save me from this Philistine'. And to Goliath he said, 'You are coming against me with sword, spear, and javelin, but I come against you in the name of the Lord almighty'. He did not want to take any of the honour to himself, he wanted God to have the glory. The story is found in 1 Samuel chapter 17.

The humility of Jesus

However, it is in the life of Jesus that we see the greatest examples of humility. Isaiah prophesied that Jesus would be meek and take humbly the opposition of sinners. He wrote, 'He was treated harshly, but endured it humbly; he never said a word. Like a lamb about to be slaughtered, like a sheep about to be sheared, he never said a word' (Isaiah 53:7). The leaders of the temple said many wrong things about Jesus. They called witnesses, who told lies about Him. Some said He had a devil inside Him. They tried to stone Him and to push Him off a cliff. But He took all these accusations humbly as Peter tells us, 'When he was insulted, he did not answer back with an insult; when he suffered, he did not threaten, but placed his hopes in God, the righteous judge' (1 Peter 2:23).

Jesus instructs us how to behave when we are insulted personally. He said, 'If anyone hits you on one cheek, let him hit the other one too' (Luke 6:29). One day a man selling Bibles came to a home where there was an atheist. When the Christian tried to sell him a Bible the atheist hit him on the face. The Christian rolled up his sleeves, and showed how strong his arm muscles were. He said to the atheist, 'I could give you a very good beating, but Jesus said that I should turn the other cheek to you'. He turned the other side of his face to the atheist, and invited him to hit again. That so surprised the attacker that he apologised and bought a Bible!

Although the Lord Jesus set us these examples of humility when He was attacked personally, He acted very differently when someone was doing harm to the Kingdom of God. When he found traders in the temple area, He took a whip and drove them out saying, 'It is written in the Scriptures that God said, "My Temple will be called a house of prayer for the people of all nations." But you have turned it into a hideout for thieves!' (Mark 11:17). When the Pharisees were disgracing God by the way they were acting, Jesus called them hypocrites because of their deceit. He likened them to snakes. He also warned sinners that they would be punished in hell.

We see then that although humility is part of the fruit of the Spirit, and that it makes a Christian meek, it does not mean that a person who is a Christian will be weak, when facing people doing evil things. They will be humble enough to admit their own unworthiness and will give the glory to God for the strength He gives them to overcome, just as David did when he defeated Goliath.

We have that illustrated in Paul's advice to Timothy. 'The Lord's servant must not quarrel. He must be kind towards all, a good and patient teacher, who is gentle as he corrects his opponents, for it may be that God will give them the opportunity to repent and come to know the truth' (2 Timothy 2:24, 25). Leaders in church organizations need humility in dealing with problems that arise in the life of the church. They must remain humble and yet strong in their discipline against sin, and those who do wrong. They must never be proud of their gifts, or the position they hold in the Body of Christ - His Church.

One time when a young minister was asked to be guest preacher in a church which did not have a minister, he walked proudly up the steps into the pulpit with his written sermon, believing that he was going to make a very good impression on the congregation, and perhaps would receive a call to be their minister. However, when he was preaching, he found that the sheets of his sermon had become mixed-up and he became very confused. When he walked down the steps from the pulpit, at the end of the service, he looked very humble. The caretaker of the church said to an elder afterwards, 'If that minister had gone up as humble as he came down, he would have come down as confident as he went up, knowing that God had helped him!' But he failed to be humble as he entered the pulpit. The impression he gave the congregation, as he entered the pulpit, was that he was quite capable of conducting a good service, but his pride came before a fall.

In 2 Chronicles 26:16-17, we find this description of King Uzziah, 'But when King Uzziah became strong, he grew arrogant, and that led to his downfall.' This meant that the priest told him, 'You have offended the LORD God, and you no longer have His blessing.' If we want to retain the blessing of God on our lives we must practise humility as a part of the fruit of the Spirit.

Questions

1. Why do you think Aaron and Miriam caused trouble for their brother?

2. What does the reaction of Moses to this trouble, show us about his character?

3. Does it mean that Moses was too weak, and afraid to stand up to his brother and sister?

4. Why was Moses furious, and did not seem humble, when he found the people worshipping the golden calf?

5. Discuss when a Christian should be humble and take abuse, and when he or she, should put up a spiritual battle.

6. Why did David not order Shimei to be killed?

7. What reason did David give for killing Goliath?

8. Do you remember how, in our last study, Peter described Jesus' reaction when He was insulted?

9. Explain what Jesus meant when He said, 'Turn the other cheek'.

10. Why did Jesus act differently when he drove traders out of the temple?

STUDY SEVENTEEN

THE HOLY SPIRIT BRINGS SELF-CONTROL

Reading: 2 Peter 1:3-9

God's divine power has given us everything we need to live a truly religious life through our knowledge of the one who called us to share in his own glory and goodness. ⁴In this way he has given us the very great and precious gifts he promised, so that by means of these gifts you may escape from the destructive lust that is in the world, and may come to share the divine nature. ⁵For this very reason do your best to add goodness to your faith; to your goodness add knowledge; ⁶to your knowledge add self-control; to your self-control add endurance; to your endurance add godliness; ⁷to your godliness add brotherly affection; and to your brotherly affection add love. ⁸These are the qualities you need, and if you have them in abundance, they will make you active and effective in your knowledge of our Lord Jesus Christ. ⁹But whoever does not have them is so short-sighted that he cannot see and has forgotten that he has been purified from his past sins.

We have now come to the last part of the fruit of the Holy Spirit as mentioned by Paul in Galatians 5:22, 23. It is SELF-CONTROL. To be a fruitful Christian we must control ourselves through the power of the Holy Spirit. In the above reading, Peter describes a number of the parts of the fruit of the Spirit, and among them is self-control.

There are four ways in which this self-control should work in our lives.

Self-control of our minds

Our mind is the part that causes us to make decisions. It has to choose between right and wrong. It allows habits to be formed in our lives. If the mind is not controlled by the Holy Spirit, it can cause bad habits to be formed, and wrong decisions to be made. That is why Paul wrote, 'Do not conform yourselves to the standards of this world, but let God transform you inwardly by a complete change of your mind. Then you will be able to know the will of God' (Romans 12:2). The Holy Spirit transforms our minds so that we can choose what God wants. Then the mind refuses to agree to the things that would grieve Him. J B Phillips in his translation of that verse writes, 'Don't let the world around you squeeze you into its own mould, but let God re-make you so that your whole attitude of mind is changed'.

That means that we must be fully yielded to the control of the Holy Spirit. Two people cannot drive the same car at the same time! So self and the Holy Spirit cannot control the same mind at the same time. The devil will continually be waiting to tempt us to think wrong things, and to do things which would be sinful, but if the Holy Spirit is in control of our minds, He will show us the way to escape from temptation. We have the wonderful promise, 'God keeps His promise, and he will not allow you to be tested beyond your power to remain firm; at the time you are put to the test, he will give you the strength to endure it, and so provide you with a way out' (1 Corinthians 10:13). We see then that the Holy Spirit must

be in control of self, then we will have self-control, as we
find in verse 6 of the above reading from 2 Peter.

Self-control of our spirits

When we have the self-control which the fruit of the Holy
Spirit brings, then our spirits are controlled, just as we
have found that our mind is controlled. Our spirits control
our emotions, and when they are not controlled by the
Holy Spirit they can cause a person to become angry,
moody, over-anxious, sad, discouraged, depressed, or
unforgiving. Then things are said and done for which a
person is sorry later! Husbands can lose their temper with
their wives, or wives with their husbands. Parents can
become cruel to their children, instead of correcting them
in love.

Jesus showed the Pharisees that although they controlled their outward lives with many rules, and appeared
holy, their spirits inside were unclean and evil. He said,
'On the outside you appear good to everybody, but inside
you are full of hypocrisy and sins' (Matthew 23:28).
Those evil spirits within caused them to hate Jesus. They
opposed Him and in the end forced Pilate to crucify Him.
Some church members can be well controlled outside,
where people can see them, but inside their spirits are not
controlled by the Holy Spirit. We read in 1 Corinthians
6:20 (KJV) 'Glorify God in your body and in your spirit,
which are God's'. We can only glorify God in the control
of our spirit when it is transformed by the Holy Spirit.

Self-control of our bodies

Our last scripture points out that we should glorify God

in our body as well as our spirit. 1 Corinthians 3:16 tells us, 'Surely you know that your are God's temple, and that God's Spirit dwells in you!' And in chapter 6:15, 'You know that your bodies are parts of the body of Christ. Shall I take a part of Christ's body and make it part of the body of a prostitute?' In Romans 6:12, 13 we are commanded, 'Sin must no longer rule in your mortal bodies, so that you obey the desires of your natural self. Nor must you surrender any part of yourselves to sin to be used for wicked purposes'. That is why we need the fruit of the Holy Spirit in our lives to enable us to control our bodies as part of the body of Christ.

Our hands must be controlled to do only the things the Lord wants them to do, and not to do anything that would grieve Him. Our eyes should be turned away from things that would corrupt our minds. Our feet should only go to the places where we can take the Lord Jesus with us. Then there is our tongue. James warns us, 'The tongue is like a fire... It sets on fire the entire course of our existence with fire that comes to it from hell itself' (James 3:6). When our tongues are not controlled by the Holy Spirit, they can gossip about other people, criticise, tell lies, or swear. Such tongues cause great trouble in the church and neighbourhood. The book of Proverbs has two warnings for us. 'Be careful what you say... a careless talker destroys himself' (13:3). 'The more you talk the more likely you are to sin' (10:19).

Then there is the question of food and drink. Our bodies need to be looked after, as they are temples of the Holy Spirit, and part of the body of Christ. It is necessary for us to control our eating habits to the things which are good for our bodies. If the things we eat or drink cause our bodies to malfunction, they will not be at their best for the use of the Holy Spirit. Self-control must be exercised when it comes to our appetites. Proverbs again has a warning. 'If you have a big appetite restrain yourself. Don't be greedy for the fine food' (23:2, 3).

Most of the medical associations of the world now tell us that tobacco smoke is one of the main causes of the deadly disease of cancer in the body. Not only does it bring the death sentence to the smoker, in many cases, but now it has been confirmed that non-smokers who live or work with smokers, also can develop cancer! It was recently disclosed by an expert, that it is estimated that 8,000 babies a year die because his or her parents smoke. This raises a very important question: is it right for a person to smoke who professes to be a Christian, and who claims that his, or her, body is a temple of the Holy Spirit? Is it right for that person to be inhaling something which, it is very likely, will destroy God's temple? To satisfy a selfish habit, is it right to be the means of bringing death to others. Tobacco is a very addictive habit, but the Holy Spirit gives the power to break the habit.

It is very sad to know that some families spend as much money on tobacco in one week as an African minister's allowance for three months! Will they have any excuse on the great judgement day? Although smoking was not known in the days of Isaiah, he asks, 'Wherefore do you spend money for that which is not bread?' (55:2, KJV).

So when it comes to seeing that our bodies are controlled for God's glory, we should be able to say with

Paul, 'But I keep under my body, and bring it into subjection: lest that by any means, when I have preached to others, I myself should be a castaway' (1 Corinthians 9:27).

Self-control of our possessions

Lastly, it is very important that the fruit of the Holy Spirit enables us to control the use of the things we possess. In a number of languages in Africa and elsewhere, there is no word for 'have'. One cannot say, 'I have a farm', or 'I have a sum of money'. One can only say, 'I am WITH a farm,' or 'I am WITH a sum of money' etc. Because when we pass away from this world we are not able to take anything with us. We are only with our possessions while we are here. The Bible makes it clear to those of us who are Christians, that we are stewards, looking after the things the Lord has given to us, so that we can use them for His glory, and the extension of His kingdom in this world.

Jesus said in the parable of the sower that the thorns which choke out the Word of God are 'the worries and riches and pleasures of this life' (Luke 8:14). If the use of the things we are with in this world is not controlled by the Holy Spirit in our lives, then they choke out our spiritual fruitfulness. Paul warned Timothy, 'For the love of money is a source of all kinds of evil' (1 Timothy 6:10). In 2 Peter 1:3-4, we read that God has showered gifts upon us, but they are given so that we may 'escape from the destructive lust that is in the world'. Someone has said that the only way to control our possessions is to 'Make all the money we can, save all the money we can, and GIVE all the money we can'. Here is a poem from an unknown author:

> Money isn't worth a thing
> Unless it helps the soul to live.
> The richest man in all the world,
> Is he who has the most to give.

Questions

1. Why do our minds need to be controlled?

2. Describe how Paul says our minds should be controlled?

3. What controls our emotions?

4. What happens if our spirits are not controlled by the Holy Spirit?

5. Why does the Holy Spirit want our bodies?

6. What does Paul mean by 'self-control', as part of the fruit of the Spirit?

7. What does the Bible have to say about our eating?

8. Discuss why tobacco is harmful to our bodies, which should be 'temples of the Holy Spirit'.

9. Why must a Christian control the use of his, or her, money and possessions?

10. What does Peter mean by 'destructive lust' in the world (2 Peter 1:3, 4)?

STUDY EIGHTEEN

SUMMARY OF THE FRUIT OF THE SPIRIT

Reading: 1 Corinthians 13

I may be able to speak the languages of men and even of angels, but if I have no love, my speech is no more than a noisy gong or a clanging bell. [2]I may have the gift of inspired preaching; I may have all knowledge and understand all secrets; I may have all the faith needed to move mountains - but if I have no love, I am nothing. [3]I may give away everything I have, and even give up my body to be burnt - but if I have no love, this does me no good.

[4]Love is patient and kind; it is not jealous or conceited or proud; [5]love is not ill-mannered or selfish or irritable; love does not keep a record of wrongs; [6]love is not happy with evil, but is happy with the truth. [7]Love never gives up; and its faith, hope and patience never fail.

[8]Love is eternal. There are inspired messages, but they are temporary; there are gifts of speaking in strange tongues, but they will cease; there is knowledge, but it will pass. [9]For our gifts of knowledge and of inspired messages are only partial; [10]but when what is perfect comes, then what is partial will disappear.

[11]When I was a child, my speech, feelings, and thinking were all those of a child; now that I am a man, I have no more use for childish ways. [12]What we see now is like a dim image in a mirror; then we shall see

face to face. What I know now is only partial; then it will be complete - as complete as God's knowledge of me.

[13]Meanwhile these three remain: faith, hope, and love; and the greatest of these is love.

We have now studied all the parts of the fruit of the Spirit - let us sum up the nine parts, as given to us in Galatians 5:22, 23. The first part mentioned is LOVE. We will now see that the other parts are ways in which love works.

Love is what strengthens joy

As we read in Nehemiah 8:10, 'The joy that the LORD gives you will make you strong'. A Christian who is joyful has much more strength to love the Lord and others. 'Love never gives up, and its faith, hope, and patience never fail,' we read in the seventh verse of the above reading in Corinthians. A person who is sad and gloomy is concerned with self and is weak in love for others, becoming impatient and depressed. Jesus linked joy and love in John 15:11, 12, 'I have told you this so that my joy may be in you and that your joy may be complete. My commandment is this: love one another, just as I love you.'

Peace gives love a strong foundation

'God's peace, which is far beyond human understanding, will keep your hearts and minds safe in union with Christ Jesus' (Philippians 4:7). It is God's peace which keeps us united in love to Christ. As we found in our study on peace, it is the referee which warns us if there is anything coming into our lives which would cause our love for Christ to become cold. We may have many temptations and trials, but in them all the fruit of the Spirit provides peace, enabling us to continue our union of love in Christ.

Patience is love holding firm

As mentioned, trials and difficulties will come, and we need patience to overcome them, as we read in 2 Thessalonians 3:5, 'May the Lord lead you into a greater understanding of God's love and the endurance (patience) that is given by Christ'. Patience and love go together. A mother who loves her child will patiently sit hour after hour by its bedside when it is ill. When we love Christ we will patiently serve Him, even when things seem to be very difficult.

Patience is needed in our love for others. 'May God, the source of patience and encouragement, enable you to have the same point of view among yourselves by following the example of Jesus Christ, so that all of you together may praise with one voice the God and Father of our Lord Jesus Christ' (Romans 15:5, 6). In our churches and fellowships we need the patience of the Holy Spirit to enable us to love one another, and to see the other person's point of view. Many times our love for others can be tested. They may not respond the way we would like. Their way of doing things may upset us, and that can hinder fellowship if we do not patiently continue to love that person in Christ. That is where we need the fruit of the Spirit, giving us love, to patiently keep the unity of the Spirit in the bond of peace.

Sometimes we can be tempted to feel impatient with

God, if He does not answer our prayers the way we wish. Job had this temptation when his wife said to him, 'You are still as faithful as ever, aren't you? Why don't you curse God and die?' But Job answered, 'You are talking nonsense! When God sends us something good, we welcome it. How can we complain when he sends us trouble?' (Job 2:9, 10). Job's love for God helped him to patiently bear his severe pain, and the loss of his family and possessions, until the time of his healing and restoration came.

Kindness is love in action

Because the Holy Spirit has given us kindness as part of the fruit of the Holy Spirit, kindness should show in our actions. It is easy to be kind to those we love with our human love, but the love of God in our hearts helps us to be kind to those we would not naturally love. We love them with God's love, and show kindness on His behalf. God's love in our hearts also causes us to love and be kind to our enemies, as Jesus commanded us, 'I tell you: love your enemies and pray for those who persecute you' (Matthew 5:44). We are told to be kind to them, 'If your enemy is hungry, feed him; if he is thirsty, give him a drink; for by doing this you will make him burn with shame. Do not let evil defeat you; instead, conquer evil with good (kind deeds)' (Romans 12:20, 21).

Goodness is love's nature

The reason the Spirit filled Christian can love and be kind to others, even his enemies, is because God's goodness has been given to him as part of the fruit of the Spirit.

Peter tells us that as Christians who have the Holy Spirit, we 'share the divine nature. For this very reason do your best to add goodness to you faith; and to your goodness add knowledge' (2 Peter 1:4, 5). It is God's nature to practise goodness. When He puts His divine nature of love in us, then it becomes natural for us to practise His goodness, although Satan will always try to hinder us.

Faithfulness is love's assurance

When a husband really loves his wife, he remains faithful to her, and is not involved immorally with other women. There may be those who will try to tempt him, of course. The same also applies to a wife who loves her husband. She will remain faithful to him even when other men are trying to seduce her. When the love of God is in a Christian's heart he remains faithful to God. Without that love, unfaithfulness can result. James warns, 'Unfaithful people! Don't you know that to be the world's friend means to be God's enemy?' (4:4). We cannot love worldly things and be faithful to God. God will always be faithful to us because He loves us with an everlasting love. Because faithfulness is part of the fruit of Holy Spirit in our lives, it is not hard for us to have faith in the promises of the One we love.

Gentleness is love being humble

Jesus said, 'Take my yoke and put it on you, and learn from me, because I am gentle and humble in spirit; and you will find rest' (Matthew 11:29). Paul wrote to Timothy, 'The Lord's servant must not quarrel. He must be kind towards all, a good and patient teacher, who is gentle as he corrects his opponents, for it may be that God will give them the opportunity to repent and come to know his truth' (2 Timothy 2:24, 25). The gentleness given to us through the fruit of the Spirit, enables us to be humble and obedient to the Lord. It causes us to treat others the way we would like to be treated. It is wrong for a Christian to like to argue harshly, and be proud of his, or her, ideas and knowledge. Paul begged the Christians at Corinth, 'By the gentleness and kindness of Christ I beg you not to force me to be harsh when I come' (2 Corinthians 10:1, 2).

Self-control is love overcoming temptation

When one has yielded himself, or herself, completely to God, and is filled with the Holy Spirit, one loves God so much that there is a fear of doing anything that would grieve Him. This causes a person to watch out for Satan and his temptations. When the temptations come, one has to use the self-control that will allow the Holy Spirit to give the power to overcome. Jesus pointed this out when He was calling people to follow Him. 'If anyone wants to come with me, he must forget self, carry his cross, and follow me' (Matthew 16:24). Carrying our cross is to choose to do things which our self does not like to do, but love for the One we are following causes us to do it joyfully.

This then is the summary of how the love of God produces the fruit of the Holy Spirit in our lives.

Questions

1. Why is love such an important part of the fruit of the Spirit?

2. How does love strengthen joy?

3. Do you remember what acts as a referee, if our love for the Lord grows cold?

4. How does a person who loves the Lord, wait for Him to answer?

5. Why are Christians kind to those who insult them?

6. What does Peter mean when he says that God wants us to share the Divine Nature (2 Peter 1:4, 5)?

7. Describe how we can only be faithful to God if we love Him.

8. Discuss the meaning of 2 Timothy 2:24, 25.

9. Explain the meaning of the words of Jesus: a Christian 'must forget himself, carry his cross and follow Me'.

10. Can you remember all nine parts of the fruit of the Spirit?

STUDY NINETEEN

GIFTS OF THE HOLY SPIRIT

Reading: 1 Corinthians 12:1-20

Now, concerning what you wrote about the gifts from the Holy Spirit. I want you to know the truth about them, my brothers. [2]You know that while you were still heathen, you were led astray in many ways to the worship of lifeless idols. [3]I want you to know that no one who is led by God's Spirit can say 'A curse on Jesus' and no one can confess 'Jesus is Lord!' unless he is guided by the Holy Spirit.

[4]There are different kinds of spiritual gifts, but the same Spirit gives them. [5]There are different ways of serving, but the same Lord is served. [6]There are different abilities to perform service, but the same God gives ability to all for their particular service. [7]The Spirit's presence is shown in some way in each person for the good of all. [8]The Spirit gives one person a message full of wisdom, while to another person the same Spirit gives a message full of knowledge. [9]One and the same Spirit gives faith to one person, while to another person he gives the power to heal. [10]The Spirit gives one person the power to work miracles; to another, the gift of speaking God's message; and to yet another, the ability to tell the difference between gifts that come from the Spirit and those that do not. To one person he gives the ability to speak in strange tongues, and to another he gives the ability to explain what is

said. [11]But it is one and the same Spirit who does all this; as he wishes, he gives a different gift to each person.

[12]Christ is like a single body, which has many parts; it is still one body, even though it is made up of different parts. [13]In the same way, all of us, whether Jews or Gentiles, whether slaves or free, have been baptized into the one body by the same Spirit, and we have all been given the one Spirit to drink.

[14]For the body itself is not made up of only one part, but of many parts. [15]If the foot were to say, 'Because I am not a hand, I don't belong to the body', that would not keep it from being a part of the body. [16]And if the ear were to say, 'Because I am not an eye, I don't belong to the body', that would not keep it from being a part of the body. [17]If the whole body were just an eye, how could it hear? And if it were only an ear, how could it smell? [18]As it is, however, God put every different part in the body just as he wanted it to be. [19]There would not be a body if it were all only one part! [20]As it is, there are many parts but one body.

We have been studying the fruit of the Holy Spirit in our last studies. In the above reading we also see that the Holy Spirit gives gifts. In this study we will look at some of the gifts given to Christians by the Holy Spirit.

Why gifts are given

The Holy Spirit gives these gifts for the common good of all, we read in verse 7, and for the work of Christian service (Ephesians 4:12). The gifts are given to enable us to produce spiritual fruit in our lives, and thus glorify God (John 15:8). They are not given to be used for selfish purposes, or to bring honour, or fame to us.

Illustrated by members of our bodies

Paul in our reading uses our bodies to illustrate how each part of the body has its particular gift. The eye has the gift of sight; the ear the gift of hearing; the nose the gift of smelling; the tongue the gift of speaking; the mouth the gift of eating; the hand the gift of gripping, lifting, writing etc; the feet the gift of walking, and the brain the gift of thinking, remembering, and controlling the other parts of the body. None of these members can change places, because each one has its own special gift, to do the work for which it has been placed in the body. Their gifts differ, as we read in 1 Corinthians 12:15-20.

Christians are members of the body of Christ (His Church)

'Christ is like a single body, which has many parts; it is still one body, even though it is made up of different parts' (1 Corinthians 12:12). The Church of Jesus Christ in this world, then, is likened to a 'body' with different parts or members. Every person who is born again, becomes a member of the body of Christ through the eternal life which is then imparted by the Holy Spirit (v 13).

Each Christian has his own work to do in the Body of Christ

As we are told in 1 Corinthians 12, the foot cannot do the work of the hand, but that does not exclude it from doing its own work. The ear cannot do the work of the eye, but it has its own work of hearing. All these members have to use the gifts given to them to do their own work so that the body can function properly. None of them can say that because it is not able to do the work of another member that it does not belong to the body (v 15).

If our left hand became jealous, and went on strike, because our right hand is always used to shake hands, and greet our friends, we would be in trouble. If our ears decided not to listen any more because they do not have such a prominent position as our nose, we would be deaf, and unable to function normally. So in the church of Jesus Christ, His body, each Christian has a special function to perform, and should not be jealous of those who have other gifts and positions.

Paul tells us, in this chapter (vv 8-11), that the Holy Spirit gives us the very gift that we need to perform the function the Lord has chosen for us. Some have the special gift of wisdom, the ability to deal with problems and difficulties in the service of the Lord. Another has the gift of extra knowledge, and the ability to teach and equip the church for more effective service. Another has a special gift of faith, bringing to the church the challenge to expect and attempt greater things for God, and not to be afraid to attack evil.

That was the kind of gift of faith David had. When all the army of Israel was crouching in fear because of Goliath, he stepped out to fight. Because Goliath was defying God, David believed that the Lord would give him power to overcome the giant. Some in the church have a special gift which gives them faith to pray for people who are ill. It is not always God's will to heal, otherwise we would never die!

Some are able to speak, or hear, in other languages, as

happened on the day of Pentecost, when people from 15 countries understood what was being said by the speaker in Acts 2.

The danger of using gifts for a selfish purpose

We must use the gift, or gifts, that the Holy Spirit gives us, to glorify the Lord. We must never use them to bring fame or honour to ourselves! In a country where missionaries of the South Africa General Mission (now Africa Evangelical Fellowship) had gone to preach the gospel, one man who professed to become a Christian, began to pray for those who were sick. Some people were healed, and he began to announce that he had the gift of healing. However, it was not very long before his pastor saw that he was showing evidences of spiritual pride, as he boasted about his gift. The pastor warned him, but instead of listening, he decided that he would show the pastor his power, by raising someone from the dead!

He found a child that had been badly burned. He put the child back in the fire until it died, and then began to pray for it to come back to life. Of course that did not happen. God was not willing to give him power to do something so foolish, just for his own fame. The police were told what he had done, and he was sentenced to many years in prison. The missionaries of his church were sent out of the country, because the government thought they were teaching him to do such things. His desire for self-glory spoiled the influence of his church.

There are also Satanic gifts

When we worked in Africa, there were people who

thought that because a witchdoctor had power to do
miraculous things, he must get the power from God. But
Satan can use his servants to perform miracles too! He
gives gifts to those who will worship him. Jesus said,
'False prophets will appear; they will perform great
miracles and wonders in order to deceive even God's
chosen people, if possible' (Matthew 24:24). John tells
us that we must try the spirits. 'My dear friends, do not
believe all who claim to have the Spirit, but test them to
find out if the spirit they have comes from God. For many
false prophets have gone out everywhere' (1 John 4:1).
Because a person is used for healings, or professes the gift
of being able to speak in an unknown language, that does
not prove beyond doubt that the gift comes from God.
Witchdoctors have power to see people healed, and when
they go into one of their trances they use many words
which are not in their local language.

Jesus said that it is by a person's fruit he is known. 'Be
on your guard against false prophets... you will know
them by what they do' (Matthew 7:15, 16). We have been
studying the fruit of the Spirit in previous studies. If a
person is not showing that fruit, and living a holy life of
love, joy, peace, patience, kindness, goodness, faithfulness, humility and self-control, then we can question his
source of power. In Revelation 13:13, 14, we read that
Satan's agent will be able to do many wonderful things,
and perform miracles.

Before leaving this subject of gifts, we should remem-
ber a very serious statement that Jesus made. He said,
'When Judgment Day comes, many will say to me,
"Lord, Lord! In your name we spoke God's message, by

your name we drove out many demons and performed many miracles!" Then will I say to them, "I never knew you. Get away from me, you wicked people!"' It is very important that we know that we have been born again, and that we have His Holy Spirit using the gifts He has given us to produce His fruit in our lives.

Questions

1. Why does the Holy Spirit give us gifts?

2. How does Paul illustrate the use of the gifts of the Spirit?

3. What lesson was Paul teaching when he said that the hand cannot do the work of the foot?

4. What happens in a church when some members get jealous of the positions and work of others?

5. What went wrong with the man in the story who prayed for the sick?

6. How do we know that Satan can also give 'gifts' which deceive people?

7. In 1 John 4:1, we are told not to believe all who claim to have the Holy Spirit, but to test them. How can we do that?

8. Does Satan try to deceive Christian by giving people power to perform miracles?

9. If a person uses the name of Jesus to claim miracles, does that prove that they are performed by Him.

10. What is required of us, then, who are branches in Jesus, the Vine?

STUDY TWENTY

THE IMPORTANCE OF STUDYING GOD'S WORD

Reading: Joshua 1:6-9

'Be determined and confident, for you will be the leader of these people as they occupy this land which I promised their ancestors. [7]Just be determined, be confident; and make sure that you obey the whole Law that my servant Moses gave you. Do not neglect any part of it and you will succeed wherever you go. [8]Be sure that the book of the Law is always read in your worship. Study it day and night, and make sure that you obey everything written in it. Then you will be prosperous and successful. [9]Remember that I have commanded you to be determined and confident! Don't be afraid or discouraged, for I, the Lord your God, am with you wherever you go.'

In the above reading, God tells Joshua how to be successful in doing God's work. God wanted him to bear spiritual fruit as he led the Children of Israel in to possess the land of Canaan. He told Joshua that he must meditate on the Word of God, day and night, so that he could be successful.

The instructions which the Lord gave Joshua are instructions which apply to all men and women who want to bear the fruit of the Spirit. We too must meditate on the

Word of God in the Bible. If a plant is to bear fruit it must be fed, by drawing nourishment from the soil, through its roots. A good farmer, or gardener, feeds the plants with compost, and other recommended plant foods. We too need food if we are to produce spiritual fruit. The spiritual food that we need is to be found in the Bible. That is why we must meditate on it day and night, as Joshua was told to do.

To meditate, means 'to chew over' in our minds the truths we find in Scripture. After a cow, and certain other animals, eat grass or other fodder, they swallow it and then lie down and chew it over again! That is how we should read the Word of God and study it. We should remind ourselves again and again of the words we have read, and go over them many times in our minds, drawing more and more of the truth they contain, by the help of the Holy Spirit. That is what God told Joshua to do.

The Bible has spiritual 'milk'

When one is 'born again' he or she is like a new-born baby. That is why Peter wrote to those who had been recently converted, 'Be like new-born babies, always thirsty for the pure spiritual milk, so that by drinking it you may grow up and be saved' (1 Peter 2:2). A healthy baby loves milk, so a young, spiritually-healthy Christian loves to feed on the Word of God. A baby does not have teeth when it is born, so it cannot chew. That is why it must have milk. A young Christian cannot understand many difficult parts of the Bible, but there is much in the Bible that is simple, and can be taken like a baby takes milk.

The Bible has spiritual 'meat'

However, a person cannot only live on milk all his life! As a child grows it needs more solid food. So it is with the Christian who is growing in faith. The writer of Hebrews warns us about the danger of not growing up, spiritually. 'Anyone who has to drink milk is still a child without any experience in the matter of right and wrong. Solid food, on the other hand, is for adults, who through practice are able to distinguish between good and evil' (Hebrews 5:13, 14).

Just as a child grows teeth and is able to chew solid food, so as a Christian matures, he must learn to chew the solid truths of Scripture. That is the way we draw strong, nourishing truths as we mature in the Christian life. If we do not eat food for our bodies, we become weak and ill. If Christians neglect to feed on spiritual food, they become weak and are unable to resist Satan's temptations. That is why Satan tries hard to keep us from studying the Bible. He tries to keep us more interested in other things, so that we will have very little time for the Bible.

We have already read about this little boy in Study 10 (page 67) and he reminds us that the Bible must not be neglected. One day when he was playing with a ball in a room in his house, the ball landed on a high shelf. He climbed up to find it, and saw a very dusty book lying on the shelf. He called to his mother, 'Mummy, do you know that there is a book up on this shelf?' His mother said that it was God's book, as she called the Bible. He then said to his mother, 'Don't you think we should send it back to Him, because we never use it'. Unfortunately that is how the Bible lies in many homes.

The Bible is a textbook

In schools and colleges, students have textbooks which instruct them on different subjects. The Bible is God's textbook to show us the way of salvation, and how to live a successful Christian life, so that we will produce spiritual fruit. Jesus said, 'Whoever remains in me, and I in him, will bear much fruit... If you obey my commands you will remain in my love' (John 15:5, 10). To bear fruit we must keep His commands. How do we know what they are? How do we know how to keep them? We can only find out if we study them in the Bible. If a student fails his examination it is not the fault of the textbook. He has not followed its instruction properly. If a Christian fails to bear fruit it is because he has not followed the instructions given in the Bible.

Paul wrote to young Timothy, 'Do your best to win full approval in God's sight, as a worker who is not ashamed of his work, one who correctly teaches the message of God's truth' (2 Timothy 2:15). The King James version says, 'Study to show thyself approved unto God, a workman that needeth not to be ashamed, rightly dividing the word of truth'. When we buy items like a radio, we get an instruction book which tells how to operate it. It is called a manual. The Bible is our manual to show us how to live a successful and fruitful Christian life. We must study it thoroughly, and follow its commands, and instructions.

The Bible is a lamp

In Psalm 119:105, it states, 'Your word is a lamp to guide me and a light for my path'. The Christian who is producing the fruit of the Spirit, is one who walks in the light which the Word of God sheds on his path. The Bible shows how to overcome temptations, and how to keep close to our Guide, through the Holy Spirit. 'I keep your law in my heart, so that I will not sin against you', verse 11 of this Psalm states.

The Bible is seed

Jesus said that the Word of God is seed (Mark 4:14). The Psalmist writes, 'Those who wept as they went out carrying the seed will come back singing for joy, as they bring in the harvest' (Psalm 126:6). We must study the Bible and store it in our own hearts, and sow it in the lives of others. Jesus said in the above chapter in Mark that some of the seed will fall on hard ground, some on rocky ground, some among thorns, but that some will fall in good ground, where it will produce an abundant harvest. It is our job to sow, and then to leave it to the Holy Spirit to make it grow. 'I sowed the seed, Apollos watered the plant, but it was God who made the plant grow,' Paul wrote in 1 Corinthians 3:6.

The Bible is like a sword

'The word of God is alive and active, sharper than any double-edged sword. It cuts all the way through, to where soul and spirit meet, to where joints and marrow come together. It judges the desires and thoughts of man's heart' (Hebrews 4:12). When Jesus was tempted by Satan in the wilderness, He used the Word of God like a sword to drive Satan away. It is only when we as Christians have thoroughly studied the Word of God that we will know how to use it to overcome Satan. Also, it will only be then that we will be able to use it, by the help of the Holy Spirit, to bring conviction to sinners, by piercing their defensive armour of arguments and excuses.

Questions

1. Describe what it means to MEDITATE on the Word of God.

2. What does Peter mean by 'pure spiritual milk' (1 Peter 2:2)?

3. What then is meant in Hebrews 5:13, 14 where we are told 'solid food is for adults'?

4. Why is lack of Bible Study like fasting from food?

5. Why is the Bible like a textbook, or manual?

6. How may a Christian know the correct way to walk with Jesus?

7. Explain how the Word of God produces fruit in a Christian's life.

8. What is meant by 'sowing and watering' the seed in 1 Corinthians 3:6?

9. What weapon did Jesus use to defeat Satan's temptations?

10. Why do many people neglect and even dislike the Word of God?

STUDY TWENTY ONE

A FRUITFUL CHRISTIAN PRAYS

Reading: Luke 11:9-13

'And so I say to you: Ask, and you will receive; seek, and
you will find; knock, and the door will be opened to you.
¹⁰For everyone who asks will receive, and he who seeks
will find, and the door will be opened to anyone who
knocks. ¹¹Would any of you who are fathers give your
son a snake when he asks for fish? ¹²Or would you give
him a scorpion when he asks for an egg? ¹³Bad as you are,
you know how to give good things to your children. How
much more, then, will the Father in heaven give the Holy
Spirit to those who ask him!'

A fruitful Christian is one who spends much time in
PRAYER. Our reading points out to us that the Lord is
waiting and anxious to give us all the things that we need
to live the Christian life, and produce spiritual fruit. Jesus
promises that the Lord is more anxious to give us the
Holy Spirit, than a father would be anxious to give
something necessary to his child. As we have been
studying, the Holy Spirit is the One who gives us the
power we need to live a holy life and bear fruit. Jesus
mentioned a number of times, the need for prayer, and
also promised that prayer would be answered. 'If you
remain in me and my words remain in you, then you will
ask for anything you wish, and you shall have it', Jesus

134

said in John 15:7. Of course, it must be understood that we will only want to ask for the things which please the Lord, and the things which help us to serve Him better. That is made clear by the fact that Jesus made the promise to those who remain, or abide, in Him. We have already studied the subject of abiding in Christ.

There is a wonderful invitation in Hebrews 4:16, 'Let us have confidence, then, and approach God's throne, where there is grace. There we will receive mercy and find grace to help us just when we need it.' We will now see that prayer has two parts.

Prayer is talking to God

Jesus said in our reading in Luke 11, 'ask'. We are told in 1 Thessalonians 5:17-18, 'Pray at all times, be thankful in all circumstances. This is what God wants from you in your life in union with Christ Jesus.' So in talking to God we ask for guidance, provision, and protection. We ask for grace to overcome temptations and for power to witness for Him. But we must also come with thanks for all He has done for us, in answering our prayers, and being our kind Heavenly Father, and showing His love for us in such wonderful ways. It is good to know that when we talk to God, it is not necessary for us to form words with our lips. He looks at the desires of our hearts, and He can read our thoughts. There is the verse of a hymn which states:

> Prayer is the soul's sincere desire,
> Uttered or unexpressed!
> The motion of a hidden fire,
> That trembles in the breast.

If we cannot express ourselves to the Lord as we would like, then Paul reminds us, 'The Spirit also comes to help us, weak as we are. For we do not know how we ought to pray; the Spirit himself pleads with God for us in groans that words cannot express' (Romans 8:26). In other words, the Holy Spirit is waiting to explain to God what we really desire in our hearts. Is that not wonderful?

Prayer is allowing God to talk to us
Many people agree that prayer is talking to God, so they will spend a few minutes asking for the things they want, and perhaps saying a few words of thanks. Then they say, 'Amen' and go off to bed or to work. They do not give the Lord any chance to talk to them! When we go to visit a well-known friend, we like to sit down and spend time conversing with him or her. Conversation is a two-way thing. We talk to our friend, but we give him or her time to talk to us. Suppose we went to a friend's house and talked non-stop for fifteen minutes. Then we said good-bye, without giving our friend a chance to say one word. Our friend would consider that our mind was seriously confused. Yet that is what many people do with God. But instead of saying goodbye, they say amen.

You will remember the story of the boy Samuel in 1 Samuel 3. He was living with the priest called Eli, and helping him with the work in the House of God. One night when the boy was in bed, he thought he heard Eli calling him. He went to the priest's room, but the priest said he had not called him. Three times that happened. Then the priest knew that God was calling the boy, so he told Samuel, 'If he calls you again, say, "Speak, Lord,

your servant is listening'". When Samuel heard the voice
again, he did as Eli had told him, and God gave him a
special message for Eli.

When we pray, and we have talked to God, then it is
good for us to say, 'Speak, Lord, your servant is listening'. But we must not expect God to speak to us with
words we will hear with our ears. We now have our
Bibles, and God speaks to us through the Bible. That is
why the Bible is so important, as we saw in our last study.
But many people just act as if they are saying, 'Listen,
Lord, your servant is speaking', then they go away
without listening for the Lord to speak to them. The
Psalmist tells us to be patient and WAIT for the Lord to
act (Psalm 37:7). To pray effectively we must be willing
to take time with the Lord in prayer. Our conversation
with Him must not be rushed.

When we want to have a serious discussion with a
friend, or to talk in confidence, we do not like to be
disturbed. To be interrupted by others, or have some loud
noise making it difficult to be heard, spoils our conversation. That is also true when we are conversing with the
Lord in prayer. Jesus said, 'When you pray, go to your
room, close the door, and pray to your Father, who is
unseen. And your Father, who sees what you do in
private, will reward you' (Matthew 6:6). To hear the
voice of the Lord in our hearts as we read the Bible, we
need to find a quiet place to pray. In some homes it may
not always be possible to find an empty room in which to
pray. Some other method will have to be used to be alone
with the Lord. Perhaps rising early, before other members of the family are around, or arranging with others to

be left alone for a time. In our next study we will be
finding out how the Lord Jesus found time, and places to
pray.

We can see an illustration of the need to be alone to
hear the voice of the Lord, from the story of a dog that was
trained to look after sheep. The shepherd was driving his
flock of sheep along a public road, when he saw a car
coming in the distance. He wanted his dog to move the
sheep over to one side of the road so that the car could
pass. But just as he began to give his dog instructions, a
little pup came out from a house and began to bark loudly.
The sheep dog could not hear what the shepherd was
saying, although it knew he was trying to give instructions. It quickly ran up on to a high bank at the side of the
road, to get away from the little dog so that it could hear
the shepherd's voice. We have to get away from the
noises of this world, if we want to hear the voice of the
Lord.

Although we have been discussing private prayer in
this study, there is also family prayer, and public prayer,
when we join with others. But public prayer is not
enough, it is necessary for us to have private conversations with the Lord so that He can deal personally with us,
and prepare us to bear the fruit of the Holy Spirit.

Questions

1. What condition did Jesus mention in John 15 must be fulfilled, if our prayers are to be answered?

2. Jesus said, 'Ask what you will and you shall have it'. What did he mean?

3. What are the two parts of prayer?

4. How can one listen to God?

5. What is the mistake that many people make when praying?

6. How do we talk to God?

7. Why did Jesus suggest that we find a private place to pray?

8. Name some other places where we should pray, as well as in private.

9. Should it only be people who pray out loud who attend prayer meetings?

10. Should we become discouraged if our prayers are not answered quickly?

STUDY TWENTY TWO

HOW SHOULD A FRUITFUL CHRISTIAN PRAY?

Reading: Ephesians 6:14-20

So stand ready, with truth as a belt tight round your waist, with righteousness as your breastplate, [15]and as your shoes the readiness to announce the Good News of peace. [16]At all times carry faith as a shield; for with it you will be able to put out all the burning arrows shot by the Evil One. [17]And accept salvation as a helmet, and the word of God as the sword which the Spirit gives you. [18]Do all this in prayer, asking for God's help. Pray on every occasion, as the Spirit leads. For this reason keep alert and never give up; pray always for all God's people. [19]And pray also for me, that God will give me a message when I am ready to speak, so that I may speak boldly and make known the gospel's secret. [20]For the sake of this gospel I am an ambassador, though now I am in prison. Pray that I may be bold in speaking about the gospel as I should.

In our last study we discussed the subject of PRAYER as a conversation with God. In prayer we speak to Him and He speaks to us through His Word, the Bible. In this study we will look at examples of prayer in the Bible. We will look at things which hinder our prayers from being answered, and we will see the importance of faith when we approach God in prayer.

Examples of how Jesus prayed

Jesus set us many examples when He prayed to His Father. Although the Lord Jesus was the Son of God, He spent much time talking to His Father in heaven. If the Lord Jesus saw the need to spend much time in prayer, how much more should we.

First of all, we find that He was willing to rise early in the morning so that He could be alone with His Father. We have an account in Mark 1:35-38, of how He got up early to pray. As we read in that chapter, He had been very busy the night before. We are told that after the sun set all the people in the town gathered in front of the house where He was staying, and He healed many and cast out evil spirits. One would think that after such a busy night, Jesus would have wanted to have a long lie in bed the next morning! But we read in verse 35, 'Very early the next morning, long before daylight, Jesus got up and left the house. He went out of the town to a lonely place, where he prayed'.

Not only did He rise early, but note that He wanted a lonely place to pray, so that He would not be disturbed. We discussed in our last study, the need of a quiet place when we want to talk to God privately. Jesus knew that He was going to have a busy day after sunrise, so He planned to talk to His Father first.

We read that it was not long before Peter and his friends were out searching for Jesus. When they found Him they said, 'Everyone is looking for you' (verse 37). If Jesus had not got out of bed early, He would not have had any time to pray. Martin Luther said that if he did not have two hours, early in the morning, to pray before he began his duties, things did not go well during the day.

Also, after a busy day, Jesus would take time to pray. In Matthew 14 we read the account of the Lord Jesus feeding the five thousand men, as well as women and children, with five rolls and two fish. He had already preached to them and healed many of them, so He must have been very tired at the end of the day. But we read in verse 23, 'After sending the people away, he went up a hill by himself to pray. When evening came, Jesus was there alone'. Although He had had a busy day He wanted time, and a quiet place, to talk to His Father.

But He was also willing to spend all night in prayer. The night before He chose His disciples, we read, 'At that time Jesus went up a hill to pray and spent the whole night there praying to God' (Luke 6:12). We need to spend much time in prayer before we have to make important decisions, as we see from this example of Jesus, preparing to choose his disciples.

A very common excuse with Christians is the statement, 'I am so busy that I do not have much time to pray'. Jesus could easily have made that excuse. Wherever He went the crowds were waiting for Him, and He had to get away from them early in the morning, or late in the evening. We even read of one time when the crowds were waiting for Him. He left them and went away to pray. 'But the news of Jesus spread the more widely, and crowds of people came to hear him and be healed from their diseases. But he would go away to lonely places where he prayed' (Luke 5:15, 16).

Most of us are busy, and it is easy to neglect to take as much time to pray as we should. But often a lot of time is wasted in needless conversations, or on other things which are not really necessary. We need to set aside a certain time, or times, each day to converse with God. If the day is very full then it will mean rising earlier or taking time before going to bed, so that our prayer time is not rushed.

Sin hinders answers to prayer

The Psalmist tells us, 'If I had ignored my sins the Lord would not have listened to me' (Psalm 66:18). That is why Isaiah warns us, 'Don't think that the Lord is too weak to save you or too deaf to hear your call for help! It is because of your sins that He doesn't hear you. It is your sins that separate you from God when you try to worship him' (Isaiah 59:1, 2). When we come to God in prayer, our hands must be free from sinful things and our hearts must be clean from sinful thoughts (Psalm 24:3, 4). That is why Jesus said, 'If you are about to offer your gift to God at the altar and there you remember that your brother has something against you, leave your gift there in front of the altar, go at once and make peace with your brother, and then come back and offer your gift to God' (Matthew 5:23, 24).

When Jesus called Zacchaeus, we see an illustration of someone seeking cleansing before his prayer is answered. The first thing he did was to confess his sins, and promise to repent, then Jesus said, 'Salvation has come to this house today' (Luke 19:9).

Jesus told the story in Luke 18, of two men who prayed in the temple. The Pharisee's prayer was not answered because, instead of confessing his sin, as the tax collector did, he told God about the good things he had been doing. And Jesus said that it was the tax collector and not the Pharisee, whose prayer was answered.

Faith is necessary

'No one can please God without faith, for whoever comes to God must have faith that God exists and rewards those who seek him' (Hebrews 11:6). 'When you pray, you must believe and not doubt at all... A person like that, unable to make up his mind and undecided in all he does, must not think that he will receive anything from the Lord' (James 1:6-8). We find then that faith is very important if we are to see our prayers answered, so that we can bear much spiritual fruit. We can only have faith if we remain closely united to Christ, and are led by the Holy Spirit in our prayers. As we have seen before, Jesus said in John 15:7, 'If you remain in me and my words remain in you, then you will ask for anything you wish, and you shall have it'. It is only when we are cleansed from sin and abide in Christ that we can have faith to believe His promise in Mark 11:24, 'When you pray and ask for something, believe that you have received it, and you will be given whatever you ask for'. That is real faith!

Questions

1. Why did Jesus get up very early in the morning to pray?

2. What kind of place did he choose for prayer, and why?

3. Do you remember some other times when He prayed?

4. When we are busy, is that a good excuse not to take time to pray?

5. Suggest how we can arrange extra time to pray.

6. What did David say would hinder his prayers being answered?

7. What reason did Isaiah also give why prayers are not answered?

8. Discuss what Jesus says in Matthew 5:23, 24 must be done, before we go to worship and pray.

9. What does James say is necessary when we pray?

10. Explain what is meant by 'faith' in Hebrews 11.

STUDY TWENTY THREE

FISHING FOR SOULS

Reading: Luke 5:1-11

One day Jesus was standing on the shore of Lake Gennesaret while the people pushed their way up to him to listen to the word of God. ²He saw two boats pulled up on the beach; the fishermen had left them and were washing the nets. ³Jesus got into one of the boats - it belonged to Simon - and asked him to push off a little from the shore. Jesus sat in the boat and taught the crowd.

⁴When he finished speaking, he said to Simon, 'Push the boat out further to the deep water, and you and your partners let down your nets for a catch.'

⁵'Master,' Simon answered, 'we worked hard all night long and caught nothing. But if you say so, I will let down the nets.' ⁶They let them down and caught such a large number of fish that the nets were about to break. ⁷So they motioned to their partners in the other boat to come and help them. They came and filled both boats so full of fish that the boats were about to sink. ⁸When Simon Peter saw what had happened, he fell on his knees before Jesus and said, 'Go away from me, Lord! I am a sinful man!'

⁹He and the others with him were all amazed at the large number of fish they had caught. ¹⁰The same was true of Simon's partners, James and John, the sons of Zebedee. Jesus said to Simon, 'Don't be afraid; from now on you will be catching men.'

¹¹They pulled the boats up on the beach, left everything, and followed Jesus.

We have been studying how to be fruitful Christians. That is God's plan for each Christian. He produces the fruit of the Spirit in our lives so that we can be witnesses (Acts 1:8). He has given us the gifts of the Holy Spirit so that we can be successful in serving Him (1 Corinthians 12:4, 5). In that way we produce fruit which brings glory to our heavenly Father (John 15:8).

Of course, we cannot see all the fruit that the Holy Spirit produces through our witness and service. We have to sow the seed and leave the Holy Spirit to make it grow (1 Corinthians 3:6). However, Jesus has commanded us to 'catch men'. When He called His disciples in Matthew 4:19, He said, 'Come with me, and I will teach you to catch men'. In the reading at the top of this study, Jesus promised Peter, 'Don't be afraid; from now on you will be catching men'. Let us see why Jesus said we should 'catch' people like a fisherman catches fish.

Fishermen must go where there are fish
One day I found our three-year-old daughter in the bathroom, holding a stick. A string was hanging into the bathwater from the stick. I asked, 'Ruth, what are you doing?' 'I am fishing,' she answered. Of course, she did not catch any fish, because there were no fish in the bath water! If we are to obey the command of Jesus to catch people who are not Christians and bring them to Him, then we must go to where there are people who do not

know Jesus. Many church members make a mistake. They think that we can only catch people for Jesus in church. But most of the people in church have already been caught, although some may be like 'dried' fish, some like 'smoked' fish, and some even like 'frozen' fish.

The people who need to be caught for Jesus do not often come to church. If we want to catch them, we must go to the homes where they live, the places where they work, the places where they spend their leisure time, and the places where they shop. Hospitals, bus and railway stations are places where there are opportunities to witness for Jesus to non-churchgoers. Jesus told His disciples, before He went back to heaven, 'Go throughout the whole world and preach the gospel to all mankind' (Mark 16:15). The gospel cannot be preached to all mankind in our churches, because all mankind does not attend church. That is why we must go and find them. We should know that the word 'preach' used by Jesus in the local language, really meant to 'talk' about Jesus.

New Testament examples of fishing for people
In John 1:40-51 we have two examples of successful fishing for men. We read about Andrew, after he had found Jesus, 'At once he found his brother Simon (Peter) and told him, "We have found the Messiah". Then he took Simon to Jesus.' What a wonderful 'catch' that was, when we remember how great an apostle Peter became, and that he brought many to Jesus during his life.

The second example in the chapter tells us how Philip brought Nathanael to Jesus. Jesus found Philip, and then

Philip found his friend Nathanael and told him about Jesus who came from Nazareth. Nathanael wanted to argue, but Philip invited him to come and see Jesus. Many times when we try to win someone for Jesus, he or she tries to argue and confuse us so that we do not challenge them to accept Christ into their lives. Philip did not argue, but brought him to Jesus! When Nathanael saw Jesus and heard Him, he said, 'You are the Son of God! You are the king of Israel!' After that, Philip continued to be a wonderful 'fisher of men'. He saw many people becoming Christians in Samaria, and he won the Ethiopian official for Jesus, as we read in Acts chapter eight.

As soon as the Samaritan woman met Jesus at the well and received the Living Water from Him, she rushed into the town and said to the people there, 'Come and see the man who told me everything I have ever done. Could he be the Messiah?' We read that many people left the town and went to Jesus. In verse 39 of John 4 we find, 'Many of the Samaritans in that town believed in Jesus because the woman had said, "He told me everything I have ever done"'. What a successful day the woman had in fishing for people. On the very first day that she was a Christian, she was used by the Holy Spirit to bring many to Jesus.

Paul found Lydia by the riverside and introduced her to Jesus (Acts 16:13-15). She was the first person in Europe to be won for Jesus by Paul. So we see that Peter, Nathanael, the Samaritan woman and Lydia did not become Christians in church. They were won, because others went out to find them!

Jesus' example of fishing for souls

We do not read of Jesus winning many followers when He preached in the temple and synagogues. It was out in the villages, towns and country places that He caught many 'fish'. He caught some of His disciples by the seaside (Matthew 4:18, 19). He found Matthew, who was also called Levi, in his office and said to him, 'Follow Me' (Luke 5:27, 28). It was at a well, that Jesus won the Samaritan woman, although He was very tired at the time. He was always ready to win men and women.

He caught Zacchaeus when he was up a tree. It is not often that one can catch a 'fish' up a tree! Jesus said that He would like to go home with him, but Zacchaeus was troubled about wrong things he had done, and he promised Jesus that he would pay back money that he had taken wrongly. Jesus then said, 'Salvation has come to this house today' (Luke 19:5-9).

As far as we can understand, Jesus was able to cause Mary Magdalene to repent at a dinner party, when other people thought that He should chase her away. If she is the woman referred to, then we read in the next chapter of Luke, that Jesus cast seven devils out of her (Luke 7:48; 8:2).

Are we going out to where non-Christians live, work, shop, travel and play, seeking to introduce them to Jesus? Or are we just sitting in our churches and expecting the 'fish' to jump out of the lake of sin and join us? A fisherman would not catch many fish if he sat on the bank of the lake or river and called the fish to jump out! If we are to be fruitful Christians, we must GO OUT and WITNESS for Jesus. Jesus said to the Christians when

He was leaving this world, 'Go, then, to all peoples everywhere and make them my disciples' (Matthew 28:19). We will discuss this in more detail in our final study.

Questions

1. What did Jesus promise would be given to the disciples by the Holy Spirit?

2. What did Jesus want the disciples to do when they witnessed for Him?

3. Is church the only place where we can introduce people to Jesus?

4. What did Jesus mean when he said 'Go into all the world, and make disciples'?

5. What lesson can we learn from Philip's success in catching Nathanael?

6. How did the Samaritan woman win the people of her village?

7. List some of the places where Jesus caught people?

8. Why are some Christians like fishermen sitting on the bank, and calling the fish to come out of the water and join them?

9. When we catch people for Jesus, what has He told us to do with them?

10. What did Jesus say shows us who are disciples?

STUDY TWENTY FOUR

METHODS OF WINNING PEOPLE

Reading: 2 Timothy 2:14-26

Remind your people of this, and give them a solemn warning in God's presence not to fight over words. It does no good, but only ruins the people who listen. [15]Do your best to win full approval in God's sight, as a worker who is not ashamed of his work, one who correctly teaches the message of God's truth. [16]Keep away from profane and foolish discussions, which only drive people further away from God. [17]Such teaching is like an open sore that eats away the flesh. Two men who have taught such things are Hymenaeus and Philetus. [18]They have left the way of truth and are upsetting the faith of some believers by saying that our resurrection has already taken place. [19]But the solid foundation that God has laid cannot be shaken; and on it are written these words: 'The Lord knows those who are his' and 'Whoever says that he belongs to the Lord must turn away from wrongdoing'.

[20]In a large house there are dishes and bowls of all kinds: some are made of silver and gold, others of wood and clay; some are for special occasions, others for ordinary use. [21]If anyone makes himself clean from all those evil things, he will be used for special purposes, because he is dedicated and useful to his Master, ready to be used for every good deed. [22]Avoid the passions of youth, and strive for righteousness, faith, love, and

peace, together with those who with a pure heart call
out to the Lord for help. [23]But keep away from foolish
and ignorant arguments; you know that they end up in
quarrels. [24]The Lord's servant must not quarrel. He
must be kind towards all, a good and patient teacher,
[25]who is gentle as he corrects his opponents, for it may
be that God will give them the opportunity to repent
and come to know the truth. [26]And then they will come
to their senses and escape from the trap of the Devil,
who had caught them and made them obey his will.

We saw in our last study that each Christian who bears
spiritual fruit, should be a 'fisher of men' (Matthew
4:19). We found that it is necessary to go out to homes,
offices, markets, bus stations, hospitals and other places
where there are non-Christians. It is not enough to sit in
church and expect them to come and join us. We must go
out and seek for the lost sheep, as Jesus said He had come
to do (Luke 19:10).

If a fisherman wants to catch fish in a river, dam or
lake, he has to use the correct bait. We know, of course,
that sometimes fishermen use nets to catch fish. That is
a picture in soulwinning when an evangelistic campaign
is conducted. At such a time there is usually a person who
has the gift of being an evangelist. But here we are
discussing how individual Christians need to study the
most effective ways of catching people for Jesus. That is
why in our Bible Reading at the top of this study Paul
urged Timothy to be a worker who is not ashamed of his
work.

The ordinary Christians are like fishermen with a rod,
line, hook and bait. They talk to individuals and must

know the correct ways to use the 'bait' which the Holy
Spirit provides. We need the wisdom which the Holy
Spirit has promised, as the King James version reminds
us in Proverbs 11:30, 'He that winneth souls is wise'.
This verse can be taken in two ways. To win souls, we
need wisdom, but it is wise to be a winner of souls!

The correct 'bait' must be used

One day, in Africa, I fished for two hours and caught no
fish. Then a small boy came along and asked me if I was
catching any fish. When I told him I had caught none, he
asked what kind of bait I was using. I showed him the
insects I had found in the manure heap in my garden. He
shook his head and said, 'The fish in this dam do not
know that bait'. He then produced a worm out of a small
tin he was carrying, and informed me that the fish were
fond of worms. He put one on my hook, and in five
minutes I had a fish. He showed me where to find some
of the worms, and I fished for another two hours and
caught ten fish! The bait made all the difference!

Many Christians are trying to bring others to Jesus,
but they are not depending on the Holy Spirit to give them
the correct bait. Often they depend on their own intellect
and arguments. Jesus said, 'When I am lifted up from the
earth, I will draw everyone to me' (John 12:32). We must
lift up Jesus and witness to His love and power, through
His death on the cross, and His resurrection, to transform
lives. It is sad that some have been members of a church
for many years, but have never had the joy of introducing
anyone to Jesus.

Jesus' method at the well in Samaria

When Jesus saw the woman coming to the well, He knew that she was a sinful woman, but he did not start the conversation by condemning her for her sins. He used water as a 'bait' to capture her interest and curiosity. Then He introduced her to the Water of Life, which He told her would satisfy the deep thirst of her soul - the thirst which she had tried to quench with immorality, and other sins. The account in John 4 does not tell us all the things Jesus said to her, because she told the people in the town that He told her everything she had done! But that was after he had captured her interest with the discussion about the Living Water. If he had started the conversation with an attack on the way she was living, she would no doubt have gone off as soon as she had drawn her water.

The Samaritan woman uses Jesus as 'bait' to catch others

When the woman received the Water of Life, she rushed to the people in the town, and said, 'Come and see the man who told me everything I have ever done. Could he be the Messiah?' And as we saw in our last study, 'Many of the Samaritans in that town believed in Jesus because the woman said, "He told me everything I have ever done"' (John 4:29, 39). If she had gone to people to attack their sinful ways, she would not have had success, but when she lifted up Jesus, many came to see Him and then believed in Him as Christ, the Messiah.

It is easy for church members to condemn sinful people, and even to scold them for their sins, but that is not a good method, if we want to win them for Jesus. We must recognise that the reason they do sinful things is because they are trying to satisfy an emptiness, or thirst, within their souls - a thirst that only Jesus can quench. Therefore we must witness for Jesus in such a way that sinners will see that He is the answer to the longings they have for satisfaction and peace. We must tell them that Jesus loves them, has died so that they can be forgiven, and is waiting to receive them.

How can we see sinners turning from their sins?

If a small child picks up something that is very dangerous, like a knife or a razor blade, a parent can have great difficulty in getting the child to part with it. Trying to pull it away may mean that the child will grasp it tighter and do itself much harm. The parent knows that the best way to get the child to give up something that is dangerous is to offer it something that it will like better - perhaps something to eat. Then the dangerous item is dropped, and while the child eats, it is removed.

Sinners love their sins, and if we try to snatch them away from their sins, they resent it and try to hold them tighter! But as we have seen, Jesus said, 'When I am lifted up from the earth, I will draw everyone to me' (John 12:32). Jesus is the true 'bait' with whom we can fish for men. It is our responsibility to glorify and lift up Jesus by our lives and by our words, so that He will attract sinners to accept Him as their Saviour.

When the Holy Spirit helps us to offer Jesus to them, and they see that He is much more attractive than their sins, they will be willing to drop their sins and receive Him. Jesus promised that the Holy Spirit brings power to witness for Him (Acts 1:8). We must draw that power through prayer and study of the Word of God, and by abiding closely in Jesus. As we saw in earlier studies, Jesus is the Vine and we are the branches. It is only when the Holy Spirit flows from Him into us that we can produce the fruit of the Spirit, and win people for Jesus.

Do you want to be a winner of souls? Do you want your life to be spiritually fruitful? Daniel tells us, 'They that be wise shall shine as the brightness of the firmament and they that turn many to righteousness as the stars for ever and ever' (Daniel 12:3 [KJV]). If we just remain nominal church members, without bearing the fruit of the Spirit, we will be like the tree that Jesus condemned because it only had leaves. My prayer is that the studies in this series will have resulted in many Christians producing more of the fruit of the Holy Spirit in their lives. And that as a result, those who have studied the series will have a number of souls to present to Jesus on that day when we all give an account of our stewardship, and how we have used the gifts He has given to us. May God grant it.

Questions

1. Discuss what it means to use the correct 'bait' in catching people for Jesus.

2. How did Jesus attract the Samaritan woman to accept eternal life?

3. What do you think would have happened if Jesus had started by saying to the woman, 'You are a big sinner'?

4. What reason did the people from Sychar give for accepting Jesus?

5. Why is a sinner like a small child with a dangerous instrument?

6. How does a parent usually get a child to give up a dangerous thing?

7. What did Solomon say was necessary if we are to win people to Jesus?

8. Where do we get this wisdom?

9. Finish these words of Jesus, 'Without Me you can do .... (John 15:5).

10. Make a list of the things you have learned from these studies.

ANSWERS TO STUDY QUESTIONS

Study One

1. Bearing much fruit (John 15:8).
2. Because it occupied space that could be used for a fruitbearing tree (Luke 13:7).
3. To teach that an unfruitful Christian is wasting space in the church.
4. It shows that God is patient, and sometimes waits for fruit. But it is also a warning to an unfruitful Christian.
5. First, we must be careful to keep on bearing fruit, and secondly, if we fail to do so, we grieve the Holy Spirit.
6. Because all the things he mentioned are part of one fruit.
7. The Fruit of the Spirit.
8. The fact that we had not attracted others to follow Jesus.
9. We should not waste it on things that do not help us to bear fruit (Ephesians 5:16).
10. Matthew 9:38 and Luke 10:2.

Study Two

1. The design of the planets etc in space, and the plan which gives us vegetables and fruit in our gardens.
2. The plan He has designed to enable those of us who are Christians, to bear spiritual fruit.
3. By surrendering our lives to Him, and asking Him to live within us as our Saviour.
4. The Holy Spirit.
5. He produces spiritual fruit in our lives.
6. Galatians 5:22, 23.
7. He is the 'Gardener', who keeps us clean, prunes, and protects us.

8. Jesus said in John 15:5, 'Without Me you can do nothing'.

9. We must obey Him (John 15:10).

10. Galatians 5:20, 21.

Study Three

1. A Christlike mind (Philippians 2:5).

2. It means that we should not allow worldly influences to shape what we do and say.

3. Our lives are transformed, because our minds are renewed and love the things Christ loves.

4. We are new persons. Old things have gone out of our lives, and new desires have taken their place (2 Corinthians 5:17).

5. A sinful nature (Psalm 51:5).

6. Because there is no other way to see the Kingdom of God, and no other way in which we can have eternal life (John 3:16).

7. He thought he had to become a baby again, and be born from his mother.

8. Jesus told Nicodemus that it was not his 'flesh', or body, that needed to be born again, but the spirit that controlled his body.

9. It is receiving a new heart, that is, the part of us that controls our will, is changed by God.

10. No. That person must choose, personally, to invite Jesus into his or her life (Revelation 3:20).

Study Four

1. Through the new birth, we are grafted into Him, and the Holy Spirit flows through us.

2. In this case the 'heart' does not mean the organ that pumps our blood. It means the centre, or heart of our mind, the part of us that controls our will and decides what we do, say, and where we go.

3. (a) sorrow for sin; (b) confession of sin; (c) forsaking sin and (d) trusting God to forgive us by believing in Jesus as our Saviour.

4. In 2 Corinthians 7:10 (KJV).

5. Worldly sorrow is sorrow for ourselves, and fear of punishment. Godly sorrow is being sorry for God, because we have grieved Him.

6. To God, and anyone else we have wronged, as in the case of Zacchaeus, who confessed to Jesus, and then promised to give back money to those from whom he had taken it deceitfully.

7. No. Proverbs 28:13 tells us that we must confess and FORSAKE our sins. However, Jesus taught us to pray day by day, forgive us our trespasses. Those are things we do, unwittingly, because of our lack of maturity, but different from keeping on doing the things that we know are sinful.

8. It means we must trust Him for forgiveness; we must accept Him as Lord and King in our lives; and we must be willing to serve Him in the fellowship of the church.

9. Yes. The Spirit of God assures our spirit that we are His children.

10. Justification means that God looks on me 'Just-as-if-I'd' never sinned, when I trust Jesus to forgive me, as He has taken our punishment for us.

Study Five

1. They hinder us from bearing fruit, as fungus weakens a fruit branch.

2. So that he would be able to teach transgressors, and sinners would be converted to God (Psalm 51:13).

3. That seems he meant sinful thoughts, words and actions.

4. Because God wants clean messengers.

5. Pride, selfish ambition, fear and jealousy.

6. They ran away when He was arrested.

7. They do not stand up for Him when people are swearing, or telling sinful stories, and many are ashamed to witness for Him.

8. He promised to send the Holy Spirit to them.

9. Because He was the One who used the disciples to witness and perform miracles.

10. They prayed and waited on God, and we expect that they confessed and asked forgiveness for the times they were proud and jealous of one another.

Study Six

1. Anger causes one to say and do things which grieve the Holy Spirit.

2. They are described as 'foolish things' (Proverbs 14:17).

3. No. Colossians 3:9 tells us that we must not lie in any way.

4. God does not bless the congregation and many members become lukewarm.

5. They were defeated, and a number of them were killed.

6. It gives those who are wronged an opportunity to condemn Christians.

7. Jesus said that it is wrong to consult false prophets (Matthew 24:24).

8. The King James version calls that fornication, and says that those who are guilty will not inherit the kingdom of heaven (Galatians 5:19).

9. Fornication is a sinful relationship between two unmarried persons; adultery is a sinful relationship between a married person and someone not his or her spouse.

10. 1 John 1:9 is one of these.

Study Seven

1. It takes away good things, which hinder us in bearing fruit.

2. Because they use up unnecessary spiritual energy.

3. Because they would hinder him, by slowing his speed (Hebrews 12:1).

4. Too much talking, visiting, playing, reading, oversleeping, etc.

5. Marriage, career, friendships, purchases, etc.

6. Money, because it leads into temptation.

7. All our money and possessions belong to God. We are looking after them for Him.

8. We must ask the Lord to guide us.

9. The more we give to God, the more He gives to us to use in His service.

10. We should be glad and willing (2 Corinthians 9:7).

Study Eight

1. Through being 'born again' (see Study Three).

2. We must present ourselves completely to Him for His use (Romans 12:1).

3. Our wills must be under the control of the Holy Spirit, only making decisions that please Him (Matthew 26:39).

4. It refers to the centre or 'heart' of our mind, because our mind influences our will, thoughts, desires, and actions (Romans 12:2; 1 Corinthians 2:16).

5. Because the Holy Spirit is Spirit, without a body, and He wants our bodies in which to live and act (Romans 12:1).

6. By submitting them to the Holy Spirit to think, say and do the things that please Him.

7. He seems to imply that all our actions should be free from unholy things.

8. The Holy Spirit wants to use them to speak His words.

9. Untruths, slander, swearing, angry words, etc.

10. Any place where we cannot take Jesus with us; places where there are immoral influences, wrong kind of jokes, or anything that would defile the mind.

Study Nine

1. When the Holy Spirit abides in us.

2. No. It is a part of the fruit of the Spirit, which influences every other part.

3. We then love others with the love which God gives us.

4. Only when our minds, wills and bodies are under the control of the Holy Spirit.

5. Because a Christian loves God, and we want to spend time with those we love.

6. That the person does not love God as he, or she, should.

7. With our human love, there are people who do not appeal to us, but the love of God in our hearts overcomes that dislike.

8. She would know that the love expressed was genuine.

People know when they are being greeted coldly, and out of duty.

9. The love of God in her heart urged her to make sure that the prisoner knew that God loved her.

10. We should also do deeds of kindness, as Jesus did.

Study Ten

1. Because part of the fruit of the Spirit is joy.

2. Many Christians do not radiate joy, so people think that the Christian life is dull and uninteresting.

3. The Bible tells us that 'the joy of the Lord gives strength' (Nehemiah 8:10).

4. 'I am here with good news for you which will bring great joy to all people.'

5. The fact that Christ had risen caused them to have fear of what would happen, but at the same time it gave them great joy to know that He was alive again.

6. Forgiveness for our sins, power over sin, eternal life and assurance of a place in heaven.

7. Give me again the joy that comes from your salvation.

8. We read that there is joy in heaven when a sinner repents (Luke 15:7).

9. Our own joy, and His joy (v 11).

10. No. They should add to our joy (Matthew 5: 11, 12; 1 Peter 4:12, 13).

Study Eleven

1. When everything is all right between us and God, through Jesus, our Saviour.

2. Because sin separates from God, and troubles the conscience.

3. It is a war between right and wrong. They know what they should do but are overcome by the temptation to do wrong.

4. When there is true repentance for sin, and a full yielding of oneself to God.

5. '...those with whom He is pleased' (Luke 2:14).

6. When we accept Him as King of our lives, because He paid the price on the cross to redeem us, and bring us back from Satan's control.

7. Through Jesus we are changed from being God's enemies to become His friends.

8. When members have not submitted to the peace of God, but are seeking their own way in church matters.

9. Hebrews 12:14. We must try to avoid doing, or saying, anything that would upset another person, unless it is a matter of conscience. Then it should be done privately (Matthew 18:15).

10. Our peace is disturbed, when we do, say, or go somewhere which grieves the Holy Spirit, just as a referee blows a whistle when there is foul play.

Study Twelve

1. He patiently waits for the sinner to repent and come to Him, as the father did for his wayward son.

2. It is like decay in natural fruit; people will reject it.

3. He was not worried, or overtaken by despair, but had faith to believe that God would answer him (Psalm 40:1).

4. They should be humble, gentle, patient, and showing love to one another (Ephesians 4:2).

5. He meant that Christians should listen to, and consider the other person's point of view, discussing it patiently without argument.

6. When we are having trials, or problems which last a long time.

7. Joyfully, with patience and prayer (Romans 12:12).

8. By studying the prophets (James 5:10).

9. Frustrated plans, illness, misunderstandings, and delayed answers to our prayers.

10. As part of the fruit of the Spirit, it is a witness and encouragement to others.

Study Thirteen

1. It is natural for human beings to be kind to those they like, but the kindness which is part of the fruit of the Spirit causes us to love and practise kindness to our enemies and those who hate us (Romans 12:20).

2. While we were yet sinners, He sent Jesus to die for us, and now gives us a place in His kingdom, and a promise of a home in heaven.

3. There is unrest, arguments, fights and even divorce.

4. They get the impression that they can only expect the same in their future marriage.

5. Bitterness, passion, anger, shouting, insults and hateful feelings (Ephesians 4:31).

6. By forgiving and praying for them (Acts 7:60).

7. We are doing it for Jesus, not for any selfish motive (Matthew 25:40).

8. By cheerfully giving tithes, talents and time to see that the needs of the church are met at home and abroad. We can also volunteer to do things like cleaning, gardening, painting and repairs.

9. By volunteering to do things which help those around us, taking interest in others' families, and always being

thankful when others help us.

10. Someone who is ill, an old person may need a visit and some jobs done, or it may be baby-sitting.

Study Fourteen

1. It is goodness in one's character which makes a person want to be kind.

2. The goodness in His character makes Him love sinners (Psalm 100). But because He is holy, He hates sin.

3. It is part of the fruit of the Spirit, which the Holy Spirit brings to us, when we abide as a branch in Jesus, the Vine.

4. The praise must go to our Heavenly Father (Matthew 5:16).

5. We are changed gradually into His likeness as we abide in Christ (2 Corinthians 3:18).

6. Goodness (Romans 12:9, 21)

7. Do not bring us to hard testing, but keep us safe from the evil one. The Lord's prayer (Matthew 6:13).

8. No. Even Jesus was tempted, but he did not sin. Temptation only becomes sinful when we yield to it.

9. The Bible promises that we will never be tempted beyond our power to find a way out (1 Corinthians 10:13).

10. They listened to Satan, instead of God (Genesis 3:4, 5).

Study Fifteen

1. It means that there is no other 'lover' in their lives.

2. By not loving anything, or any person, more than God.

3. He calls it spiritual adultery (James 4:4 [KJV]).

4. Hebrews 13:5. He says, 'I will never leave you.'

5. It is God's love poured into our lives (Romans 5:5). When we love Him, we do not find it difficult to be faithful, and do what He wants.

6. It is because Satan hates God, and does not want us to serve Him.

7. By getting us to love worldly things, and also using his servants to laugh at us, criticise us, and tell false stories about us etc.

8. He used Scripture to rebuke Satan, but took patiently the insults (Matthew 4 and 1 Peter 2:21-23).

9. He says that He will be ashamed of us when He comes back again, with the angels in the glory of the Father (Mark 8:38).

10. When he said three times that he did not know Jesus.

Study Sixteen

1. It appears that pride caused them to be jealous of their brother, and so they were not humble enough to take second place to Moses.

2. He was humble, and did not get angry or upset.

3. No. It needed more courage to take their opposition humbly, than to get angry, and boast of his position.

4. It was because the people had sinned against God. When people opposed him, Moses was humble, but when they sinned against God, he stood up and defended God.

5. When opposition and abuse are aimed at the Christian, humility is part of the fruit of the Spirit, which enables one to forgive, but when the attack is against God, then He must be defended.

6. Because his curses were against David, not the Lord (2 Samuel 16:12).

7. He said that Goliath was defying God.

8. He did not answer back, or threaten, but trusted humbly in God (1 Peter 2:23).

9. He meant that we should not retaliate if personally insulted, but should even be willing to take more, rather than get angry.

10. They were sinning against God, by using His temple for their own business (Mark 11:17).

Study Seventeen

1. Because it is the part of us that decides what we do, say and think.

2. He says that we must allow the Holy Spirit to transform our minds, so that He will be in control, and cause us to do the things that please God (Romans 12:2).

3. Our spirit controls our emotions (1 Corinthians 2:11).

4. We can become angry, moody, over-anxious, sad, discouraged, depressed, and unforgiving. We then fail in our witness for God.

5. The Holy Spirit wants our bodies, so that He can use our tongues to speak His words, our hands to do His work, our minds to think His thoughts, and our feet to carry His messages.

6. We must control our 'selves', by continually submitting to the Holy Spirit, as the manager of our lives.

7. 'If you have a big appetite, restrain yourself. Don't be greedy for fine food' (Proverbs 23:2, 3).

8. According to the medical profession it has the power to kill.

9. Because each Christian is a 'steward' and must look after these for God.

10. He points out that God has given us such wonderful gifts that we should not lust after worldly things, but share God's nature.

Study Eighteen

1. Because without love all the other parts could not survive.

2. We always have joy doing something for someone we love.

3. Our inner peace is disturbed.

4. With patience, just as a mother sits by the bed of a sick child waiting for its recovery.

5. Because the love of God in their hearts enables them to love their enemies.

6. As God is good, we are to share His goodness, by loving and serving others.

7. Illustrated by a husband and wife.

8. The servant of God must not get involved in heated arguments, but must gently teach, instruct and correct.

9. We must be willing to overcome selfish desires, and do the things that please God, even if they are difficult, because we love Him.

10. Galatians 5:22, 23.

Study Nineteen

1. To enable us to bear spiritual fruit, and glorify God (John 15:8; Ephesians 4:11, 12).

2. By showing how each member of our body has its own gift, enabling the body to function, so church members have different gifts.

3. He was pointing out that each member of Christ's

body, the church, has his, or her, own work to do, so our gifts differ.

4. The church is divided and cannot function properly, and the Holy Spirit is grieved.

5. He became proud, and took praise and glory to himself, not the Lord.

6. Jesus tells us about these in Matthew 24:24.

7. Jesus tells us in Matthew 7:15, 16.

8. Yes, as Jesus warns us in Matthew 24:24.

9. Jesus tells us that on the Judgment Day people will claim that they cast out devils in His name, but they will be told by Him, 'I never knew you' (Matthew 7:22, 23).

10. We must be fully surrendered to the Lord, and use the gifts He gives us for His glory.

Study Twenty

1. To take time to think it over very carefully, like an animal chewing cud.

2. As babies cannot chew meat, so young Christians need simple lessons from Scripture.

3. As a Christian grows spiritually he, or she, needs to meditate on more deep passages of Scripture.

4. One becomes weak spiritually, just as the body becomes weak with lack of food.

5. It is our source for 'correctly teaching the message of God's truth' (2 Timothy 2:15).

6. God's Word is a lamp to show us the way (Psalm 119:105).

7. Jesus said that the Word of God is like seed that produces fruit (Mark 4:14, 15, 20).

8. Seed of the Word of God is planted by hearing it,

watering is when help is given to understand its meaning.

9. He used Scripture.

10. Because it cuts into their consciences and judges their thoughts and actions, convicting them of wrong.

Study Twenty-one

1. We must remain in Christ and allow His Words to abide in us.

2. If we abide in Christ, then we will only ask for the things that please Him, and He will be glad to answer.

3. Prayer is a conversation with God, talking to Him and listening.

4. By studying His word.

5. They spend all the time talking to God, and don't listen like Samuel.

6. Not just with our lips. God knows the desires of our hearts, and if we cannot express them, the Holy Spirit helps us (Romans 8:26).

7. So that we would have as little disturbance as possible, and be able to concentrate.

8. There should be family prayer, and also meetings for united prayer.

9. No. Saying 'amen' means one is agreeing to what is being prayed.

10. David said, 'I waited patiently for the Lord's help' (Psalm 40:1).

Study Twenty-two

1. He knew He was going to have a very busy day, so prayed before dawn.

2. A lonely place, so that He would not be disturbed.

3. In the evening, all night, and in Gethsemane.

4. No, Jesus went away to pray when He was very busy (Luke 5:15, 16).

5. By pruning the time we spend in conversation, visiting, reading, sleeping, etc.

6. Hiding his sins (Psalm 66:18).

7. Sins separate from God, and He does not hear (Isaiah 59:1, 2).

8. We should try to sort out any misunderstanding between us and others.

9. Unless we believe the promises of God, we will not receive answers.

10. We should trust the promises of God when we have no evidence, apart from His Word.

Study Twenty-three

1. Power to witness for Him (Acts 1:8).

2. To 'catch' people and introduce them to Him (Matthew 4:19; Luke 5:10).

3. No, many of the people we want to catch do not come to church.

4. He meant to go into all the world around us - homes, workplaces, schools, shops, hospitals, markets, etc.

5. Not to argue, but introduce people to Jesus.

6. By praising Jesus, and inviting them to come to Him.

7. At a well, up a tree, in an office, at a party, and by the sea.

8. They sit in church and call people to come and join them.

9. We are to teach them to become disciples.

10. They must be bearing fruit (John 15:8).

Study Twenty-four

1. We must use the correct method to make Jesus attractive to people.

2. By using water, Jesus introduced her to the 'water of life'.

3. In all probability she would have been angry and rushed away.

4. Because of what the woman said to them (John 4:39).

5. Both of them do not know the danger of the things with which they are playing.

6. By offering something the child likes better, so we must show sinners that Jesus is much better than their sins.

7. We need to be wise.

8. By abiding in Jesus, and letting the Holy Spirit control (John 15:5).

9. Without Me you can do nothing.